The Sav

Tales from Legal Practice

Richard Barr

SOLICITORS JOURNAL

Cover image by David Haldane (who has been illustrating Richard Barr's stories for almost as long as Richard has been writing them)

Layout by Susie Bell, www.f-12.co.uk

Printed by Canon (UK) Ltd, Cockshot Hill, Reigate, RH2 8BF, United Kingdom

ISBN: 978-1-78358-304-1

A catalogue record for this book is available from the British Library

DISCLAIMER
This publication is intended as a general guide only. The information and opinions it contains are not intended to provide legal advice. The publishers bear no responsibility for any errors or omissions contained herein.

Published by ARK Group, a division of Wilmington Plc

The company is registered in England and Wales with company number 2931372 GB. Registered office: 6–14 Underwood Street, London N1 7JQ.
VAT Number: GB 899 3725 51.

To my wife Kirsten (who also features in these pages), along with my children Sophie and Nick, and my step children Becky, Bryony, Tom and Philippa

Preface

Long before I met Richard Barr I had come to admire his humorous musings on life in private practice which generally provided light relief at the end of the Solicitors Journal. Here was a man of a certain age dedicated to looking after his clients but constantly tripped up by the eccentricities of those clients, his pet animals or modern technology. He was clearly an interesting chap with some unusual hobbies; not many people own their own fire engines. One article in particular always stuck in my mind; his beautiful depiction of his father and his father's career as a local solicitor as he described the day they buried him. Telling how most of his clients were friends and most of his friends were clients will have resonated with many more solicitors than me. And how his father, rather than claiming he was a war hero, always reckoned that his war injury had helped his fly fishing. When I finally met Richard upon his joining the Law Society Council it became clear that here was a kindred spirit. A contented man with an irreverent view of the quirks of life as a small town solicitor tempered with, on occasions, a little innocent mischief. And Council was not spared as he picked up on the foibles of Council Members and some of the quaint practices as we try to manage a growing profession in an increasingly technological age. I have no doubt whatsoever that you will enjoy this welcome volume of his 'greatest hits', sometimes chuckling, sometimes laughing right out loud.

Joe Egan, president of the Law Society of England and Wales
September 2017

Contents

Contents

Introduction

This little volume is a very small selection from the four hundred or so articles I have written in *Solicitors Journal* over the past 40 years – a time span long enough to see lawyers' offices change from something not dissimilar to those described in Dickens's *Bleak House* to the present day when most firms (but not all) have fully embraced modern technology.

I had set out to do for solicitors what James Herriot did for animals. Sadly, solicitors are generally not furry and do not have tails that wag, so it will never be possible to create the oooh and ahhh factor for members of our profession. Nonetheless I hope that I have been able to show that solicitors are human even if you cannot always cuddle them.

I have frequently made personal reference to people I worked with and these included Colin, my vegetarian partner, Deborah the gin and tonic partner, Jean-Ann from Jamaica, John my bearded partner and Maureen who was my secretary and life support for most of the 25 years of the first part of my career at the original firm (Dawbarns). The book is also dedicated to them and to other colleagues who tolerated my occasional references to them. It is especially dedicated to the memory of John and Maureen who are no longer with us.

When I started writing these pieces, computers were a rarity, dictating machines were not universal and telephones still had dials rather than push buttons. Secretaries still practised shorthand (my father – who died in 2005 – see *Death of a father* – never used a dictating machine, nor for that matter a mobile phone or computer). We did not get a fax machine until the late 1970s and in the late 1990s I was still badgering the managing partner to put a computer on the desk of every fee earner.

It was not just technology that changed. The pace and pressures increased enormously – as is perhaps reflected in my harassed accounts of going on holiday (see *The Lord Chancellor on water skis*). Being a lawyer was never a licence to print money, but it was easier to make a comfortable living 40 years ago than it is now and we were less constrained by the yoke of regulation. Nonetheless I believe we served our clients well despite the fact that we did not have a rule to cover every move we made.

I fear for the future of those who are called high street solicitors (even though in reality most firms could not afford high street prices these days). They are the general practitioners and most people's gateway to access justice. They – we – are under constant attack from commercial and government forces, combined with huge increases in court fees and the year-on-year reduction of public funding for legal cases, so that our once fiercely independent profession is deprived of much of its weaponry to fight for the people we try to represent: all a far cry from when I nearly brought the Milk Marketing Board to its knees with a telephone call as described in *Goodbye Norfolk* (see page 19).

In the 1990s I somehow became entangled in a number of high profile cases. I have done no more than give the occasional glimpse of them in these pages, but they did set me on an uneasy career path that took me away from the relative comfort of the firm in which I was a partner for 25 years (and but a few months before I was to become the senior partner – see *Goodbye Norfolk*) into other firms and other cultures in an endeavour to service the claims that were beyond the resources of my original firm. In terms of career progression the move was pretty disastrous but it took me inside three different firms in seven years before I returned to my old firm but now the bottom of the pecking order (see *The savage poodle*). That eventually did not work out because just as I became settled in, the recession of 2008 hit and I was out on my ear – as described in *Fired!*. That set me, at the age of 60 in another career direction when I joined the present firm, enabling me to work from home (*Down Under but not out*).

Throughout I kept up my writing with *Solicitors Journal* – where even the setbacks provided inspiration.

Inside, you will find I have covered a random selection of topics, from spitting Americans to paragliding, from being abducted by aliens to reflecting on the antics of Bill Clinton, from a close encounter with the Queen to dealing with smiling sheep in the depths of winter and from corpses in deed boxes to a cat that came back from the dead.

This book would never have seen the light of day without the encouragement, support and guidance of Jean-Yves Gilg, the Editor-in-Chief of *Solicitors Journal*, to whom I shall be forever grateful.

Enjoy.

Richard Barr
May 2017

Chapter 1:
The day the office became a film set

Originally published 29 April 1994

I have sympathy for both sides. The trouble with solicitors' offices is that there is no clear division between the shop floor and the public relations and personnel departments. Worse than that, like some primæval stew, they are all mixed together. Within the chaotic pressures of a working day one has to try to achieve a balance between the need to get the job done and the desire to create an atmosphere where people give their best.

We used to have an open-door policy. There was once free access for all except when we were seeing clients. But that was when there was a comfortable gap between income and overheads, when you could clear your backlog in a matter of hours and when, even, you went home on Friday and did not return to the office till Monday.

Now we are all increasingly bad tempered, under pressure and unlikely to take kindly even to a visit from the friendliest face in the office. One by one, our open doors have come to remain closed; few now work with them open.

The unhappy industrial tribunal hearing in April involving a dispute between two solicitors, Mr Aaron and Mr Taylor, over the issue of whether the latter should or should not have kept his door open is, in a way, a paradigm of life in the nineties: an employer who wants an open and friendly office, and an employee under pressure who wants to work.

Those conflicts came together recently in our office with the intervention of a deus ex machina. The BBC decided that the area around our office represented Dickensian England. This autumn's costume drama series will be *Martin Chuzzlewit*. We will be watching it carefully.

During the summer, some men in anoraks were seen to be taking a keen interest in our buildings. We pondered whether to call the police or invite them in. If they were burglars, we could show them we had nothing worth stealing. The burglars claimed that they were from the BBC and were looking for suitable locations for a film. We showed them all the places we thought they ought to film: our cellars, my vegetarian partner's Linda McCartney photographs, my untidy room.

But they had other ideas - and returned some weeks later with more men, this time in expensive anoraks. How would we mind, they asked, if they took over the office for a couple of days?

And the clients too? we asked eagerly. No – we could keep the clients. And so, in between the snows of Easter, three sides of the office had all signs of the twentieth century carefully expunged from them. Wires were removed or disguised and the white painted windows were rendered black. We committed a minor breach of the Solicitors Practice Rules by sharing our premises with someone not from a learned profession. The south west corner of the building sprouted extra walls and became a shop front for: ANTHONY CHUZZLEWIT & SON DRY GOODS.

A further breach of the rules was committed at the front of the office when a new brass plaque was erected denoting that we were a fictitious international bank. Art was indeed imitating life, because in the nineteenth century the building (still known as Bank House) housed Gurney's bank (later to become Barclays). In 1879 a partner in the bank had to dash to Norwich to bring back gold to reassure customers and prevent a run on the bank.

As the day for filming drew near the streets filled with sweeps, barrow boys, whelk stalls, fruit stalls and artificial manure. Inside, wooden floors were laid over our boardroom carpet and several thousand pounds' worth of oriental antiques arrived to lend an air of unaccustomed opulence to the room.

The film crews and actors arrived. And then came a new office policy: the open window policy. If anyone was missing, they could almost certainly be found on the top floor. At least their bottoms could be found. The rest of them was sticking out of the windows looking down on Sir John Mills, Elizabeth Spriggs, Julia Sawalha and Keith Allen. For hours on end street life sprung into ACTION on the word of the director before he shouted CUT, and out came the 20th century: people in anoraks and the cigarettes.

Courtesy of the BBC, our open-door policy gave way to a closed gate policy. Along with the crumbling masonry of our listed building, we acquired a fine set of wrought iron railings and gates. One of the scenes you will be watching in the autumn is of several top-hatted men fighting to get through the locked gates of the Anglo Bengalee bank. They were so vigorous in their efforts that we had to tell them to calm down or the gate really would have been broken.

A large crowd gathered to watch. We could not tell whether it was to see the filming or the spectacle of what appeared to be a posse from the Solicitors Complaints Bureau trying to intervene in our practice.

Too soon it was over. The cobblestones were rolled up, the carriages driven away, and the actors moved out of our reception. The shop front was dismantled, and the brass plaque was taken away. All we have to show for it is a little manure ingrained in our carpets (we have not checked if it is real) and a scratch on our boardroom table which should send the BBC scurrying for that well-advertised number for a French polisher in the Yellow Pages.

And now the gates remain open, the windows are closed and the doors... well curiously more of them are open at the moment. You never know, the next group of men in anoraks might be talent spotting for extras.

Chapter 2:
The Lord Chancellor on water skis

Originally published 22 September 1995

To start with, it is very raw. You are over-tired, over-anxious and tense. It is Sunday. You have already postponed your departure from the office three times. Eventually in panic you gabble some instructions on to tape in the hope that your long-suffering secretary will have sixth sense and do something with the fish files before you get back. (I learn from John Grisham's latest book that a fish file is the kind of file we all have: the longer you leave it the worse it stinks.)

You arrive home after the last deadline to find the rest of the family lined up at the garden gate with all suitcases, rucksacks, snorkels and beach mats. You are allowed five minutes to change before joining the traffic on August's busiest weekend and beginning the slow trek to Gatwick.

As you drive you think of all the things you meant to do but in the maelstrom of those last hours you forgot. You telephone a colleague who does not appreciate having his Sunday afternoon interrupted by a hysterical solicitor. You beg him to issue the writ/exchange the contracts/register the debenture. In the background you hear a shrill voice: "Who is it dear?" The line goes dead.

You try again when you arrive at your homogenised hotel. You obtain an unobtainable tone. You sleep a fitful night, full of grim images of shouting judges, menacing officials from the Solicitors Complaints Bureau and swirling clouds of files. You are woken before dawn and check in three hours before your flight is due to leave. Has anyone ever caught a holiday flight from Gatwick that was scheduled to take off after 9 am? My theory is that having tormented tens of thousands of passengers with an early start, a long wait and an indifferent breakfast the whole airport closes down for a siesta until the return flights start to arrive at the end of the day.

The plane takes off. On the flight, you think of about 17 more things you did not do. You land and disembark palely, under the deep tanned stare of those who are going home.

You want to telephone at the airport but you do not understand the Greek instructions. Besides, you are momentarily even more distracted by the fact that your three suitcases are nowhere to be seen, even though everyone else has collected theirs and all that is left is a badly tied cardboard box and a faintly familiar luggage label.

At length there is the sound of hooves and another cart of suitcases is offloaded to some gentle braying. You rush to catch up with the crowd.

You give up trying to make further contact with the office that day and have your first drink. But no sooner is the Mediterranean sun above the horizon the following day than the impulse to communicate revives. Not far from your villa is a public telephone, but it is a card phone. There is a helpful sign in the nearby kiosk that they sell phonecards. You point to the sign. The man puts down his cigarette and informs you that he will not have any until the week after next, but you can get them in the main town 10 miles away.

Your family insist that one of the reasons why you came on holiday was to allow them to remember what you looked like. You feel trapped but the sun begins to feel good and you slowly subside into a sunbed where, in due course, you become a fetching shade of pink. You cool off in the sea and think of only one more catastrophe you did not deal with.

On day three you wake up early and catch the first bus while everyone is still asleep, returning triumphant an hour later with a phonecard with a picture of the Acropolis on it. You carefully remember to dial the extra digit and after many crackles and pops you are rewarded with a recorded announcement that calls to five figure numbers in Leighton Buzzard should be prefixed with an extra 7 (interesting but not helpful as I was not trying to ring anyone in Leighton Buzzard). Your card goes down by three units.

Your next attempt connects you with a nice German lady. You have incorrectly dialed Munich (20 units). At the third try you get through. You speak to your vegetarian partner just long enough to establish that he is not pleased to hear your voice, when two Greek ladies loudly join in the conversation and defeat any attempt at further discussion before your units run out.

You give up, have a drink and expose yourself to more ultraviolet light. The following day the urge to communicate is still with you. You start to get up to catch the bus. The sun is warm. The cicadas are rasping. The sea is blue and inviting. Maybe you will try later.

But you don't. Instead you watch the watersports in the bay, and wonder idly what the Lord Chancellor would look like on water skis. You imagine five appeal court judges being towed very fast in rubber rings behind a speedboat, their wigs and robes flapping in the wind. You feel that the long inflated banana would be a suitable method of transport for the law lords.

Then you forget all about the office, the law and Greek telephones, until two weeks later, depressed, anxious, and peeling, you step over mountains of files and pick your way to your desk. Your vegetarian partner gently breaks the news that a writ has been served on you, and he cannot find the file. You fervently wish you could be transported back to the Mediterranean beach to run a watersports centre for tired judges and never come back.

Chapter 3:
Rage about a lost file

Originally published 6 October 1995

For Shakespeare it was Love's Labour, and he penned a play about it. For Bill Bryson it was a continent, and for Conan Doyle it was a world, and they wrote books about them. It put Beethoven in a rage, and all over a coin. For me, it was a file.

It was my first day back at the office after an eventually relaxing holiday. I was greeted with the news that a writ had been served over a transaction that had been completed many years earlier.

Before my return there had already been a massive search for the file, but they eventually gave up.

If it is your own file that has gone missing there is a feeling that you must be responsible for it. I decided therefore to track it down before getting back into my work. I started by looking in all the right places: the filing cabinets, the pile of files waiting to be archived, that interesting collection under my secretary's desk.

When that did not yield fruit I started a more meticulous check: the card index (it was pre-computer), time records (to find when the file had last been worked on – ah a bit of hope here: it was only this year) or under the office kitchen sink.

Still no sign. I remained quite calm. We had had no fire or flood. A file is too big for the shredder. In theory it should still be in existence. I also knew that it was yellow. To help at times like this, we each have different coloured files.

The next step was all the filing cabinets. We have 47 in the office, each with four drawers. That involved making the noise *'swish, clunk'* 188 times, but to no avail.

I started to become tense. I had already lost two chargeable hours in this exercise. I thought I might have missed it first time, so I went through my own filing cabinets again, looking under the files and between them. I diverted my assistant to the hunt. She too went through my filing cabinets. We peered behind them. We took a drawer out to see if the file had leapt into the void beneath. It hadn't.

A trickle of sweat ran down my back. Had it been archived? The card index said not, but sometimes systems do not always work.

The archived files for the whole firm are stored in a massive cellar beneath the United Reformed Church opposite our Wisbech office. We drove there in tense silence, obtained the key to the dungeon, and plunged beneath the street.

Stepping over piles of files that did not quite make it to the shelves, we made our way to the King's Lynn section – narrow corridors between rows of files stretching from floor to ceiling, all neatly ordered and all looking depressingly similar.

If the file was down here it was not where it should be; we had to check every one of them. I found my past cases floating before me: Mrs Jones re tooth, Mr Smith re parrot, Mr Jenkins re neighbour's toilet. Twenty years of problems which had sufficiently vexed people to see a solicitor, all mouldering in a damp cellar.

But no missing file. During our quest there were muffled footsteps above us, then the distinct sound of a funeral service. It seemed entirely appropriate.

Drained, damp, dusty and demoralised, we returned the key to reception and were given a reviving coffee by John my ex-bearded partner. (He's still my partner, but he no longer sports a beard.) Outside his room was a tantalising pile of yellow files. Impossible that the file would have fled to the wrong office surely, but need to check just in case...

Alas no. As we drove grimly back to King's Lynn I reflected on previous hunts for missing items: the wills, the sets of title deeds, a wig, and the photographs of Percy's ear, which he had had bitten off in a fight.

But these musings did not help find this file. Darker thoughts began to take shape. Had the file changed colour or been stolen? Could someone (perhaps an insider) have removed it so as to make our task of defending the claim impossible?

I once more did the rounds of the office. Every cupboard, every drawer, every hole was peered into. The day had been lost, and still there was no file. I became locked in repetitive action, searching the same places again and again.

I then developed a hunch that it must be in my secretary's room. There was no way of finding out till after she had left. She was still suffering from my holiday and was in no mood to receive the suggestion that perhaps somewhere in there might be lurking the said file.

I waited until she was safely on her way home, then used the same technique employed by the police when seeking a murder weapon. I scanned every inch of her room. My search led me to her cupboard that contained stationery, an interesting piece of lingerie, a year-old calendar, several prehistoric dictating machines, some of my swimming trunks and a plastic box festooned with Christmas decorations. It seemed that once again I had drawn a blank. But what the hell – I might as well rummage among the Christmas decorations while I was there. Suddenly the walls of the office shook to a loud shriek. Nestling among the decorations were five files including the missing one.

You must now be on the edges of your desk wanting to find out if I had cocked anything up. Well, for all I know you might be the plaintiff's solicitor, and I'd hate to spoil your fun, so you'll have to find out for yourself.

Chapter 4:
Spitting lesson

Originally published 3 May 1996

The rain was breaking out in fitful showers. The old lime trees on the village green dripped nonchalantly onto those who huddled under them. Brightly coloured umbrellas sheltered brightly coloured anoraks. Arc lights fizzed in the wet. A deep rumble of thunder presaged another downpour.

Two tourists, seated by the village sign, frowned at their maps, turned them upside down and then sideways. Nowhere could they find LYTCHMERE, but that was what the sign said, so it must be right. They should have realised. After all, the village shop was displaying eggs for 6d (six old pence) per dozen and had a board on the wall offering the *Daily Telegraph* for 1d. Besides, even though this was deepest Norfolk, the village bus and the local cars must have seemed unusually antiquated.

If the tourists had waited long enough all would have been revealed. As soon as the September rain let up, a loudspeaker boomed 'ACTION' around the village of Castle Acre and old vehicles spluttered into life, while half the villagers, attired in wartime clothes began to stroll in leisured fashion according to prearranged instructions.

We were gathered that damp weekend to watch the filming of location shots of the BBC's Easter spectacular about a clash between American and British air forces in the tragic comedy (or comic tragedy) *Over Here*. Our village had been renamed, but The Ostrich, which features as a haven for the release of tension in many of my articles, remained the same.

The war caused television aerials to be removed, modern houses to be masked and Ford Sierras to be banished.

The film skips to the present day. The opening and closing shots feature Fleet, our beautiful golden retriever, towing my daughter Sophie, while my son Nicholas races back and forth on a mountain bike ostensibly delivering papers.

Over Here was fun to watch, and the children now think they will have careers on television rather than in the law, thank goodness. I liked the contrast between Martin Clunes and Sam West, and the conflict with the Americans.

But it is all very true to life. I have lived it for, well, let's just say the whole of my life. Americans have been arriving at my parents' house ever since, a little injudiciously, my father decided to end the Second World War by marrying an American from Nebraska.

My parents' first visitor was her mother to check up on what this Englishman was doing with her beloved daughter. She was accompanied by her 14-year-old granddaughter Ginger, to whom we shall return in a moment, and they were also in the process of acquiring a small baby from Ireland, who was to be taken back to Nebraska for adoption and in due course to become my cousin Kelly.

My mother took a little time to tune in to the niceties of British society. Once, when in the presence of an elderly Dawbarn, she described a small baby as a 'cute little bugger' and nearly ended my father's career.

Curiously she found the true Fen folk easier to understand than those who regarded themselves as being higher up the social scale. Their language and its inflexions were not unlike American.

As children we became quite used to an American mother. If she was given a cold stare when asking in a hardware shop for a washer for a faucet we would translate that it was for a tap. If she told the garage that she had a flat, we would say that was not where we lived, but could they repair the punctured tyre in the boot.

American cars do not have boots. They have trunks. When the family was on holiday in the USA we crossed into Canada. The border guards asked to look inside the trunk, but my father glibly announced that we did not have one. He was almost arrested for impertinence, as the officer moved towards the rear of the car with a crow bar.

The arrival of American visitors was always a moment of excitement. They would loudly enter the front door in their plastic raincoats uttering expressions like "Gee!" and "Say, isn't this cute". They would wear clothes which even in our youth we perceived might be slightly tasteless and they would drain the bottles of whisky and laugh their curled laughter way into the night.

Sometimes they would entertain us. There was an eccentric music teacher who became drunk one night and waded into one of the drainage dykes. She was up to her waist in black water and mud, and had to be rescued by two farmers using the same techniques as for extricating straying cattle.

Once the mayor of a small American town thought he was all alone. Observed by my brother William and myself from the safety of our tree house he spat one of the world's largest gobs of phlegm across the lawn.

It must have travelled 50 feet before it landed. We treated him with a lot of respect after that and introduced at every opportunity the language of expectoration, in the hope that he might attempt to beat his own record. We talked about spitting images, Spitfires and spitting in the wind. He would not do it again.

Those things happened years ago, but the latest Americans arrived last week. There was Howard, and Kendall, and Alberta and Ginger. Ginger was no longer 14 or ginger. The proceedings were sedate. The guests were polite about English lawyers. They had to be: there were several of us. The tree house has now been cut down. Nobody fell into ditches and nobody spat. But the Americans talked about life in a condom and I sat wondering whether being divided by a common language could cause schizophrenia.

Chapter 5:
Inventing the future

Originally published 17 May 1996

It is like the distant throb of a pneumatic drill or the faint odour which wafts up to my window from the Ouse at low tide. It gradually impinges on the consciousness, until you slowly realise it is there. Thus the word *Internet* found its way into my vocabulary and then, like the smell of mud from the river, wafted into my room.

In a remarkably short time since the idea was first mooted in the office, my computer now has the world at its keyboard, and I am more knowledgeable about ferrets than I have ever been before. I have visited Legoland without leaving my desk, and I have dropped in on the homes of people I certainly do not want to meet in real life.

I am a little dismayed at how unreceptive to modern technology we are as a profession. At a meeting last summer, a gaggle of local solicitors revealed that almost none of them had really got into computers in a big way.

I do realise that I have to pick my words carefully these days. A report in *The Times* at the end of last year revealed that in one month more than 4,000 connections were made at Oxford University to an Internet erotic media group. When I talked about getting into computers I did not mean that. The world is changing (again). Sometimes I subscribe to the view (expressed by some pensioners when we went over to decimal coinage) that 'they' should let the old ones die off before inflicting more innovation on the world. But I have to admit that I find the developments in technology exciting.

The Internet has been described as a huge leap for democracy, opening up unimagined possibilities of communication between human beings around the globe.

I am not convinced that the Internet will save the world. I am sure that prying governments could devise a means of tuning into what we are all saying, especially as it is all in writing and could be sucked out of the system and used in evidence against us. My hope would be that boredom would set in long before MI5 reached my seditious remarks. Alternatively, at the rate that the Internet is growing, it would take half the population to keep up with what the other half is doing. Big Brother may be watching, but at least the unemployment problem would be solved.

The Internet already is proving to be a wonderful communication tool.

Perhaps I had better give a short lesson for the bewildered (from a recently ex-bewildered). The Internet is a huge sprawling computer information exchange. It appears to be owned by nobody and everybody. If you have a modem (a black box which connects the computer to a telephone line) and pay a modest monthly subscription to a service provider, you can bring the world to your back door and take your back door to the world. Using the search facilities (quaintly called search engines) you can home in on almost any subject that takes your fancy, all for the price of a local telephone call. In seconds you can be browsing documents held on computer in America, all Europe or even Russia.

I needed a copy of the Woolf Report. Nowhere could I find it in this country. Eventually I tracked it down on the Canadian judges' web page (computer people like odd expressions). Less than five minutes later it was safely loaded on to my computer ready for me to rewrite it if I wished.

We needed to contact an American scientist who had apparently made some interesting discoveries over Gulf War Syndrome. We knew his name, a little about his work and the state he was in. Cranking up a search engine we were presented with half a dozen hits which led us straight to the scientist. It took about two minutes. Five minutes later I had sent him a message, but he did not reply for several hours. You cannot blame the Web for that: he was sound asleep. It was 3 am in the USA when he received my email.

I slipped in another expression there. Email is short for electronic mail. It is like a computerised version of the DX. Like DX, you have to go and get your messages. Unlike DX, you do not have to put your coat on and walk in the rain to a rival solicitors' office. You can stay dry as you tell your computer to check its messages, which you can read off the screen, print out or even save on disk for a rainy day.

Replying is remarkably easy. Tell the computer you want to send a reply and it automatically enters the details of your correspondent's number on the page ready for you to add your enlightenment.

One of the oddities about email and the Internet is the method of creating addresses, which often looks as though it is a random collection of letters, numbers and symbols. They may look odd to us, but I am told that computers find them every bit as riveting as Bide a Wee, Acacia Avenue, Castle Acre, Norfolk.

I am going to use the word erotic once more. A friend bought a guinea pig and wanted to know more about its needs and desires. We interrogated the Internet, and soon found ourselves in Hawaii where we were able to download pictures of guinea pigs doing what guinea pigs have been good at for millions of years.

But my search on the Internet for the word 'solicitor' was disappointing. One 'engine' produced 27 references, but only two were exclusively British. Come on you guys, let's surf the Internet, produce home pages, find out about ferrets and visit a world of virtual reality.

Chapter 6:
Beware smiling jurors

Originally published 11 July 1997

As the lights in the British empire begin to fade over Hong Kong, and the lights in a basement court in the Royal Courts of Justice persistently refuse to fade, I want to try to shed my own light on American juries.

What do Vera Chubb, Martha Hite, John Candelaria, Ruth Meier, Mike Leeper, David Gilger, Diane Faircloth, Doug Carr, Roger Brown, Tonya Stedman, Jim Osgood and Fred Clarke have in common? As the news is two weeks old now, most people will have forgotten (if they ever knew) the names of the jurors in the trial of Timothy McVeigh. You may have forgotten his name too but you won't if I remind you that he is the Oklahoma bomber.

We know their names because, after they had pronounced their verdict, they immediately became famous – for at least 24 hours.

In this country, anyone who so much as asks a juror what he had for lunch is likely to be carted off to the Tower of London and fed to the ravens. But after the McVeigh trial was over, all twelve jurors appeared on national television in the USA to chat about what they were thinking and, no doubt, to say what they had to eat.

All this is vaguely interesting to bored tourists trying to find something worthwhile on American television. But it is the stuff of which ecstasy is made for jury consultants.

We do not have such creatures over here, but in any big jury trial in the USA they are now regarded as essential. They are employed to help in the selection of juries, and in monitoring their performance afterwards.

Juries have to fill in questionnaires giving details of their background, attitude towards police, experience of suing, and being sued. They are then examined by the lawyers, who hope to pick a winning team. The problem is that a winning team for one party is definitely a losing team for the other.

During jury selection, the one thing to avoid at all costs is the smiling juror. A smiling juror really worries the jury consultants. These jurors, I am told on good authority, continue to smile throughout the trial and then deliver a verdict against the client.

Juries do not say a lot after they have been selected, so jury consultants have to work out what they are saying when they are not speaking.

Every gesture, every itch scratched, every shifting of the buttocks on a hard seat, is noted and interpreted. It is better to have the juror looking relaxed and facing you, than cross-legged and looking the other way.

Juries are used much more widely in the USA than they are here. Their use in personal injury cases ensures that victims receive compensation at a level which in this country is achieved only in libel verdicts.

It is of course well established under English law that those who lose limbs or are grossly disabled as a result of the fault of another should pull themselves together and be thankful for their £2,500 (Compensation Recovery Unit free) damages, while if somebody should suggest for a moment that a politician is bonking his secretary that is worth a million for starters.

The upholders of these great principles of law are, of course, judges. What we need in this country therefore is Judge Consultants (or JCs as they will become known): skilled experts who will assist in the selection of the right judge, and having done so, will keep a close eye on him or her throughout the trial to ensure that the case is being presented in the best possible light.

JCs will soon learn to discern the judicial body language. "Proceed with your address if you must...", "Mr Bailey, is there any point to your line of questioning?" and "I have never seen such a badly pleaded case since I was being suckled by my wet nurse" are all indicators that the judge is not on your side, as are a pursing of lips or loud and persistent sighs.

Sometimes technology gets in the way of these subtle forensic approaches, as happened this week deep in the bowels of the Law Courts where they keep those subterranean courts for the use of moles and people of a nervous disposition.

A plaintiff expert was trying to give some complex evidence and needed to use a slide projector.

"Ooo, I don't know about that," said the court enquiry official. "We don't have anything like that."

The solicitors persevered, tracked down a projector, obtained permission for its use and set it up in the court. Everything worked nicely until:

"Can we turn the lights off?"

Long silence. The problem is that these courts do not have light switches. The only way of plunging the court into darkness is for everyone to stand motionless for 15 minutes. Then if a whisker is moved, the court is bathed in glorious light for a further 15 minutes.

JCs would have some difficulty in interpreting the mood of a judge who had to wait for 15 minutes only to be extinguished (in the nicest possible way).

The solution (eventually) was for the main fuses to be pulled, but the court electrician had to be on hand to put them back again at a moment's notice in case the court caught fire, or the judge wanted the advocates to see him looking bored.

In the meantime, those JCs who sit through slide shows in court might find that they see little of the face, except the smile. And a smiling judge should be avoided at all costs, because he will still smile as he dismisses your client's case, orders you personally to pay the costs, and for good measure sends you to the Tower.

Chapter 7:
Goodbye Norfolk

Originally published 13 March 1998

A quarter of a century ago, wearing jeans and hair which did not contain a single streak of grey, I presented myself at the fledgling office of Dawbarn Barr & Knowles (as we then were, before we decided to opt for the more pronounceable Dawbarns) which nestled not altogether comfortably behind the offices of the Norwich Building Society.

"Can I help you?" asked Maureen, the only permanent member of the office staff.

"Yes I'm starting work here on Monday"

Maureen gave me a Norfolk look. In a fraction of a second and without any words it conveyed thoughts and concepts like: "Oh my God", "Look what the cat brought in", "Shall I resign or give it a few weeks?" and "I do hope he's got a suit to wear".

Twenty five years later, Maureen burst into tears when she heard that I was going.

The years between have been a blur. The beginning was optimism: wrongs to right, battles to fight with still unflagging zest.

A few days after I had arrived (yes, I did have a suit) I was visited by a milkman who had had his round taken away by the Milk Marketing Board.

With absolutely no idea about the law of milk rounds I set about bullying the board. As people are apt to go elsewhere pretty quickly for their pinta, instant action was necessary. My mention of a High Court Writ to the local manager ensured instant communication with the area office. My recollection is that by mid-afternoon the matter had skirted the regional office and was in the hands of head office.

My threats had similarly advanced. I had made a list of all the different types of injunction I could glean from our outdated copy of the White Book.

As these were the days before faxes, all the menace that I could muster had to be down the telephone. I set them a deadline of 3pm to reinstate the milk round. As the hour hand swept round, I telephoned with news of the further interesting procedures I was about to initiate.

Fortunately my bluff was not called and they capitulated at 2.55. My bill for that activity (including the days of negotiation which followed) was £50 – and I don't believe I was ever paid.

Other skirmishes followed. Often the more trivial the subject matter the more interesting the combat. Thus I would spend days in a forensic challenge to the validity of a single pair of double yellow lines, battling over the custody of the matrimonial dog or adapting the Sale of Goods Act to apply to a parrot without tail feathers.

The office grew inexorably and with each bulging of the seams we moved on to a larger building experiencing in the process floods, fire but no pestilence.

And with the buildings came the people who have provided inspiration (or at least perspiration) for these pages:

My **gin and tonic partner** started as she intended to continue, taking her full quota of holiday, (unlike the rest of us who made a virtue out of confining our recreation to the occasional day off at the weekend) and never leaving after 5.15 except in case of extreme urgency. Elegant and always beautifully manicured she has always been the despair of us the workaholics because she seldom fails to meet her target and almost never shows the least sign of sweat on her brow. But then she wouldn't would she?

Nepotism is always alive and well. He was engaged to the daughter of my optician (who happened to be a client). What better introduction could you have to my **bearded partner** when he applied to us for a job?

My **Jamaican partner**, between singing snatches of "Island in the Sun", would regale us with accounts of bizarre and eccentric treatment by the men of Norfolk to their womenfolk. The more distasteful the behaviour, the more she had to tell us how shocked she was about it all.

He was a student, had run into the back of a car and damaged his girl-friend. We sued him in a friendly sort of way on her behalf, and obtained for them both enough money to pay the deposit on a house, thereby launching him into the world of capitalism. Afterwards he came to spend a day at the office, and he never left. Successive buildings have become ankle deep in apple cores. Thus was born my **vegetarian partner**.

And came the other players, like those who have at some time or other been my secretary until they were wheeled away by men in white coats.

After the early idealistic years I settled down, bought a foreign car and kept mainly out of trouble, but I reckoned without Mrs Grey catching the ferry across the river Ouse and arriving one day damp and suffering from photosensitivity. Her complaint about Opren, unwittingly launched my career on a trajectory which has now sent it (with the influence of other gravitational forces) out of Norfolk and into the giddy excitement of Camden Town just a mile from where I used to live as an impoverished articled clerk.

A further full circle has been brought about by the change in logo of the *Solicitors Journal*. My other job (to fill the back pages of the *Solicitors Journal* with something which has nothing at all to do with law) was launched when I wrote for the late lamented *Law* magazine. And who published it? No prizes: Sweet & Maxwell, the new proprietors of the *Solicitors Journal*. So, beggin' your pardon sirs, nice to have you back.

And that just leaves me to say to you all at Dawbarns: you may think that you are safe from further revelations now that I am moving to Camden Town, but if I cannot find a vegetarian, a man with a beard or a decent feminist, I shall come back and write about you, so don't think you're off the hook yet.

Note to the 2017 book edition of this article: at the time the original article was written, Richard Barr was about to become a partner with Hodge Jones & Allen. Solicitors Journal *also had a new owner following the acquisition of the FT law & tax list – Longman's former legal publication portfolio – by Thomson-owned Sweet & Maxwell.*

Chapter 8:
Strapped to a Turk

Originally published 31 July 1998

I am still not sure what made me willingly jump off a six-and-a-half thousand feet mountain. I was already as terrified as I thought I could be. We had just experienced a hair-raising drive in an elderly Land Rover along a precipitous track with a sheer drop at every corner. As we swayed and lurched, the Turks who were to be our guides and pilots made hearty jokes about the serious injuries they had suffered from the exploits we were about to endure. The pine glades and the goats of the foothills were left behind as we wove and circled, the tyres struggling to keep us on the track. The trees began to disappear, and all that remained was a moonscape.

Even though the temperature was 35°C at sea level, the last snow had evaporated only a month earlier. With a final lurch we rounded a bend on a ridge which seemed no wider than the truck. At the top of the mountain was a solitary concrete building, a primitive loo, a bulldozer and a bored soldier with a gun.

We piled out of the vehicle and the Turks started to unfurl some very flimsy pieces of canvas.

Earlier we had (while still at sea level, and feeling relaxed, warm and safe) succumbed to the allure of soaring like a bird. Then it seemed a good idea. Then, we were reassured by the representative that they had not had a single accident this season (a little cautious when you think about it. What about last season and the one before?), and that the operation was fully insured by a reputable English insurance company. Then we had not been on the mountain passes, seen the bulldozer or the soldier with a gun.

Now it all ran counter to advice we would give clients. Now straps were being applied to our legs and leather thongs wound round our waists. Now there was a steep slope in front of us which ended in nothingness in twenty five yards. Now we were being strapped to a Turk with a proximity and intensive use of leather one expects to see only in unusual solicitors' offices.

Now we were being told to wait till the wind got up, and to be prepared to run like crazy.

"You see," said Selim to whom I was unwillingly bonded, "we have to take off like any plane. You need forward motion or you fall." Now it was little consolation that he would fall too if I did not run hard enough.

Now there was a whoosh, and some shouting in Turkish. Did I just imagine it, or was the soldier now pointing his gun?

Everything in me wanted to go back, to sit at my desk in the office and not annoy anyone, not even judges, for the rest of my life. But to do so would have shown cowardice. And would have involved a return journey along the mountain tracks. And how would the soldier with the gun have reacted?

Up, up and away

Like a mouse picked up by its tail my feet were still running long after I had been yanked into the air. In the rush I nearly lost a shoe. It was several minutes before I felt safe enough to reach down and slip it back on.

It took many more minutes before I was confident that I was not going to plummet to the earth onto the rocks hundreds of feet below me.

We had seen the parachutes a few days earlier. From a distance they looked like flying toenail clippings little curved shapes in the sky. But nail clippings do not take wing and wheel like birds.

"Never in a month of Sundays..." I thought to myself. But it was my birthday and SHE felt I needed to rise above it all. Besides, the day was Saturday.

What goes up must go further up

"We go up" announced Selim. That did not seem to be necessary. The world was already tiny beneath my feet. I was more interested in finding the shortest and safest way down. Until then I had thought that the real characteristic of parachutes was that they would deliver you gently to earth if your plane crashed or you found some other reason to be hundreds of feet above the ground. Nobody had told me about thermals and updrafts. Like eagles we gently circled until even our mountain was small below us. We were now high enough to encounter airplanes and large birds with big beaks and ugly faces.

Just when I thought we were going to go into orbit, we stopped turning and seemed to float motionless. Suddenly Selim started to struggle. My heart sank, even though the parachute did not. Was he dying behind me? What could I do if he was?

We lurched to the left, and then to the right. Then all of a sudden a hairy arm appeared in front of me. To the arm was attached a small video camera.

23

"You smile!" he commanded. I was not about to disobey. I smiled and smiled to keep him happy. I smiled at the ground to stop it rushing up at me. I smiled at the wind to stop it blowing the parachute inside out. I smiled at the miniature houses beneath and the toy cars and clockwork people as they slowly grew and transformed into the real world. I smiled at the sea which we suddenly started to swoop over, and I smiled at the beach which we effortlessly landed on, depositing me in a papal position ready to kiss the ground.

"Was it fun?" she asked. "Yes" I smiled. And having been through that experience I shall never be scared of a Master or judge again. I shall just smile, rise ten thousand feet above the court room and disguise myself as a toe nail clipping.

Chapter 9:
Clinton's lore

Originally published 25 September 1998

It was a strange sight, wasn't it? He may not be the most powerful man in the world, but as I write this he is still the leader of the most powerful country. And there he was looking small and nervous answering (or not answering if one is to be more precise) intimate questions about his sex life (sorry, one must get this right, about his un-sex life) from a high-profile lawyer.

His demeanour was the same as any defendant in a tight spot in any witness box the world over. He was uncomfortable, uncertain and almost visibly wincing as each new question was put to him.

There were no cheering crowds to give him encouragement, no White House Aides (at least none in shot) to steer him away from danger or to whisk him away from the podium if the going became too hot.

He addressed his interrogator as "sir", something even hardened criminals do not do in this country.

If we thought he was a God beforehand, we knew after those hours of questioning that he was (and here I mean "is") a mere mortal whose throat gets dry when he is under pressure and who shares the same need as we all have to empty his bladder from time to time.

Intense debates no doubt took place on Monday night as *Solicitors Journal* readers throughout the land sat on their sofas glued to the television watching a wholly new concept of legal interpretation being introduced into our culture.

Division was probably not so much along party lines:

"We must do what is right for the country, so okay let's lynch him" [Republicans].

"Oh, it was nothing serious. Anyone can make a mistake" [Democrats].

Here it was more likely to be:

"Look at him, the slimy toad. He cannot even answer his name without being evasive and smirking" [the female response].

"He that is without sin among you, let him first cast a stone..." [a view from the other gender with the help of the Bible].

"That's typical. You men are all the same..."

Leave aside for a moment what happened in the Oval room. Most family lawyers have heard about far worse from their clients as every imaginable domestic appliance is brought into play in the name of sexual gratification. My erstwhile Jamaican partner would frequently come into my room, eyes round with wonder and pour out a messy description about what HE (it is usually the men) did with the vacuum cleaner, an electric toaster or the parrot.

The cigar will no doubt be added to that famous candy bar and the more famous swimming pool as part of the natural history of sexual scandal.

But we will move on. The tabloids will provide us with new (and more exciting) titillation. President Clinton will either struggle on, somehow facing down the knowing looks he will get wherever he goes, or he will resign and perhaps go back to his old job as a professor of law. And if he does, he might well start by writing a glossary of new meanings for old words. This will be of assistance in judicial systems the world over and enable lawyers to add a new perspective to forensic enquiry.

Here is how we might get to the truth in the Clintonesque era:

"And were you driving the car at the time of the collision"

"No"

"And when you say 'no' do you actually mean 'yes'?"

"Yes and no"

"So you are now denying that you were driving the car"

"It depends on what you mean by driving. I was in the car sitting behind the steering wheel with my feet on the pedals while it was moving along, but I wasn't driving it."

"What were you doing then?"

"Well you have to put the matter in perspective. In the times before cars, nobody drove them. They drove oxen and geese to market. Now, nobody is suggesting that I had a cow or a goose in the car, so I was not driving was I?"

"You were in the car which ran over Mrs Jenkins were you not?"

"Now it depends what you mean by 'in'. In my day we used to go to inns for a drink, and you're a barrister and you went to the Inns of Court for those long boring meals. That's what I mean by the word. Clearly the car was not a pub and it certainly was not full of barristers so I must have been somewhere else and I certainly was not driving."

"But you said to the police officer afterwards that you were sorry that you ran over Mrs Jenkins and that you were driving."

"No I did not. My vocal chords may have constricted and produced a vibrating noise but I do not remember saying that."

"Are you now denying that you said that?"

"I don't remember."

"But you have just been voted Mr Memory Man 1999."

"Well I had a lot on my mind. I was running three countries. If I did remember, I have forgotten. And if I have forgotten then obviously I did not say it. So, no."

"Meaning 'yes'?"

Judge: It is quite clear that this man is totally innocent of the charge. This prosecution should never have been brought. Mr Barr you are therefore sentenced to three years' imprisonment for the offence for which I have found you not guilty.

Chapter 10:
Haunted by the law

Originally published 9 April 1999

Our first thought was that it must be the ghost. I am not a ready believer in ghosts, but those I live with (the people not the ghosts) are not so sure. Rumour has it that our old Norfolk house has seen at least one murder, and that one of Norfolk's lesser known massacres took place in the road outside (known as Bloodslat road).

A succession of visitors have said that they have 'felt' something or even heard voices when they were completely alone in the house. One of the children reported that he had seen someone walking downstairs into his room, even though there were no stairs. A builder working in the attic confirmed that there had indeed been stairs there at some time in the distant past.

One of our neighbours claims that he has been able to commune with the spirits who have been able to tell him much about the history of the house.

Yet in the face of this apparently overwhelming evidence I have remained as sceptical as any boring solicitor when faced with suggestions of the paranormal: it doesn't add up. It is not in the text books and you would never get it past a judge.

I was therefore irritated a few weeks ago to be confronted by a phenomenon which I could not explain. We had, earlier in the evening been stripping wallpaper from a downstairs room. After a stressful day at the office, stripping wallpaper is one of the milder ways of releasing tension. Others include hurling crockery, kicking the cat and murdering mothers-in-law.

Whether the stripped wallpaper released ectoplasms or disturbed restless spirits I cannot say. What I can say that there were more noises than usual outside and inside that night: bangings and bumpings and slightly ghoulish howls (which I still maintain were owls copulating). These could all be accounted for by natural phenomena.

What was less easy to account for was the sound of footsteps on the landing at 3.30 am. It was distinctive and persistent – the sound of a child pacing the floor and uncertain whether to enter. We were not asleep. We both heard the noise. I leapt out of bed to investigate. And nobody was there: everyone else in the house was sound asleep.

I am determined that there is a natural explanation for what happened, but so far it has eluded me. No one was there. Burglars had been locked out. There was no earthquake that night.

So when I encountered the next phenomenon I was beginning to feel unnerved. Ghosts do of course feature in the law. Sometimes solicitors ask in preliminary enquiries if a house is haunted.

First there has to be a description of my briefcase. It is a microcosm of my world. It contains the working papers I need in case I am stranded on a train. It is also my reserve filing system. Anything without a home seems to gravitate to my case. It houses emergency supplies: treasury tags, a calculator, some powdered drinking chocolate, half a packet of throat lozenges, several assorted paper clips, a pair of toe nail clippers, a small pair of pliers and some rust penetrating oil. It often contains essential documents for the following day's appointments.

On the night in question the briefcase had been hurled down by the front door. I cannot now remember if I murdered the mother-in-law after that or simply burned down a row of houses. Either way I slept well and there were no noises outside.

The following morning, we awoke to find a trail from the briefcase to the downstairs loo. What seemed to be mud formed a series of small loops. On the line of the trail, there was a littering of paper clips and pieces of chewed paper.

The "mud" was also spread throughout my briefcase, and had formed a rim along the edge of an original affidavit which was due to be shown to a High Court Judge later in the day.

Closer examination revealed that a corner of one of the exhibits to the affidavit had been chewed off.

Digging deeper we discovered the remnants of the pack of chocolate powder.

And all of a sudden it began to make sense. Invariably some of the springtime crop of small furry rodents make their way into the house. To them, a briefcase bulging with irresistible objects beats risking life and limb from an assault by owls any night. Here was a comfortable box that provided not only useful objects (I am sure that mice can find several good uses for treasury tags) but also a feast of chocolate. The only problem was: how to get it from brief case to nest, and this accounted for the trail – it was chocolate powder.

It was not going to be easy recounting to his lordship why he was presented with the world's first chocolate flavoured affidavit but how could I explain the other problem? From the middle of a tightly bound bundle one of the exhibits had gone missing.

Well, would you like to tell a judge that it had been spirited away by a ghost?

Chapter 11:
Eaten up with political correctness

Originally published 4 February 2000

The sad story of a lawyer who was eaten by a lion brings out a jumble of thoughts ranging from cautionary tales to political correctness. It also gives me an opportunity to bring back the essential ingredient to all decent legal stories: the animal dimension.

I am sure it is entirely politically incorrect to make light of the fact that Sergio Montella, a lawyer from San Donato in Southern Italy was eaten by his own lion. He had not been seen for a week, and all that was found were his rubber boots and a smile on the face of his tiger. I did not get that wrong. He kept tigers and a panther as well, according to a report in the Manchester Evening News. But naughty Signor Montella did not have a licence, so no doubt the authorities concluded that he received his just desserts – or at least the lion did.

Lawyer lovers will undoubtedly berate me for seeking cheap laughs at the expense of the departed, but, well, it was a long way away. I doubt if the circulation even of a mighty organ like the Solicitors Journal will reach into the innermost recesses of San Donato, so I am taking a chance that Incensed of Italy will not be swamping the editor with howls or even roars of protest.

But that does not stop me having my little howl of protest – at this new era of political correctness. PC has been around a long time, but it seems to be getting worse. Some years ago (through no talent of my own, but merely because no one else would do it) I headed up the local Citizens Advice Bureau. I was indeed the chairman, but because one must be PC I could not have that title. Missives from head office were always addressed to me as "Dear Chair" – until I objected to being referred to as an item of furniture, and particularly that item of furniture. The implication is obvious: if I am referred to a chair, then I am something to be sat upon. Due deference would suggest that I should be a more significant piece of furniture. "Dear Tallboy" or "Dear Grandfather Clock" would be more apposite. If they really wanted to demean me they should have called me "bed" or "carpet".

Sometimes political correctness can cause problems. Judges have been male for so long that they have, in a sense, become neutered (I mean the expression: "judge", and no disrespect to any of our learned judiciary). Thus when Counsel assembled not long ago before Mrs Justice Smith, they addressed her as "my lord" for the first two days of the trial until she pointed out to them that they could, if they wished, acknowledge the existence of female judges.

What really brought this to a head for me was the news report that in the name of political correctness the expressions AD and BC may be replaced by CE (Common Era) and BCE (Before Common Era). According to one press report, the Home Office has raised the possibility of a change to the new nomenclature. No doubt a commission will be set up and a few million pounds will be spent on looking into the issue.

If you look hard enough at any common expression you can find in it problems with political correctness. Take a few common grocery items:

Cheese. The federation of purveyors of cheesy products is likely to object strongly to references to hard cheese or cheesy feet. These would represent a severe slight on those who work so hard to produce pure soft cheese.

Milk. Those, on the other hand whose job it is to provide our daily pinta take grave exception to reports of funds being milked by the latest transgressing politician. And to allude to a "cash cow", is just to insult Daisy who has devoted her life to providing life giving fluid for each bowl of cornflakes.

Beef has, of course, been in the news but those having to struggle with the French and BSE do not want to hear of people beefing about their lot in life, or being expected to beef up their act.

So yes, let us make sure that the expressions we use do not offend, but let us not go to such extremes of gender and religious neutrality that we rob our language of colour and vitality, and leave it with the consistency and excitement of a tub of lard (and, please, I do not want the Lard Makers' Federation coming after me for berating their product).

Which brings us, with all the logic of non-sequitur, to the animal kingdom. A story reached me this week of a junior member of staff in a big firm by the name of Stickleback, Carp and Roach (or that is what I will call them to protect the guilty) being given a slight dressing down. The firm was, she was told, like a pond and in it there lived various life forms. As you advanced in the firm, you went up the food chain, but for the moment she should realise that she was an amoeba and if she tried to be anything else she would be engulfed without a trace.

But that might give scope for politically correct advancement in firms. This is always a tricky area, with sensitivities running high. Yet a clear stratification, with sharks at the top and primitive life forms at the bottom, would give all the scope we need for making sure that everyone is kept in his (or her) place. Thus if you were a plodder, and destined to go nowhere fast you could be promoted to toad. The racier members of the firm would be designated as salmon, whilst litigators could be crabs, crawfish and lobsters. The senior partner would be the walrus and me, well I'm just an old trout.

It was nonetheless unkind to the entire species of amoeba to compare them to humans and I have no doubt that amoeba rights activists will be after me along with everyone else I have named, including the Society for the Preservation of Wellington Bootly Challenged Partially Digested Italian Lawyers.

Dated 1 February 00 AC (anno Cherie). If I had written this four years ago the date would have been BT (before Tony).

Chapter 12:
Say Aaaargh

Originally published 21 July 2000

"But he did not even wear a white coat," my elderly client complained. She was bitterly disappointed – not because she had received a negative report from a consultant who was considering her somewhat extravagant symptoms, but because she saw him at his house, in his kitchen and he did not look like a doctor. He had no stethoscope, no interesting instruments, no ferocious receptionist, no out of date copies of the *Readers Digest* and above all he was not wearing a white coat. In short, he did not look the part.

Doctors generally have the edge over us. In spite of recent setbacks (Shipman, Ledward and the like) doctors enjoy adulation and popularity, the like of which solicitors only dream of. In the favourite people charts, doctors are invariably near the top, and solicitors stay resolutely at the bottom, along with estate agents, car dealers and traffic wardens.

Almost every glossy magazine has a chatty column with a doctor and every new twist in healthcare is faithfully commented on by medical men peering over their half lenses into the pages of national papers.

But do we attract the same attention? Sometimes, if we offer enough advertising, local papers will grudgingly publish a piece urging people to make wills. More often there will be articles complaining that as a profession we are too expensive, too slow, too complicated, too ineffectual, too self-interested and too fat.

Unless we are plaintiff lawyers in the US tobacco litigation or are commercial solicitors in the city, we are certainly not fat. Just think about those claimant lawyers and the fees they will get if they pull off those damages in the tobacco cases. Ponder, for a long moment on 40 per cent of $145 billion. That is, give or take a little, £40 billion – the sum paid to at least ten thousand National Lottery winners, enough to keep the National Health Service going for around six months, or to keep us all in legal aid for about five years.

For those fees I would be prepared to risk being a tad unpopular, but just in case they don't come my way, or yours, we need to examine ways of becoming as popular as doctors. What, indeed, do they have which we don't?

Is it because we have to charge for our services, but NHS doctors don't? I think not. Legal aid solicitors seem no more popular than those who deal with private client work.

The problem with our image is not about money. It is about how we present ourselves and what we offer. So, let us invent a new breed of popular solicitors. Everyone and everything has changed names. So must we. We have already borrowed in part from the medical profession. Our elderly colleagues are dignified with the style of 'consultants', and we have paralegals. We are also accused of ambulance chasing, but what about the middle ground? We need a nomenclature which contains a whiff of antiseptic and conveys the comfortable reassurance of the consulting room.

We need to copy the techniques of the medical profession. When clients are shown into our rooms, it is quite clearly inappropriate to offer them tea or coffee. In future, the first move must be to ask them to open their mouths and say "Aaaargh". We should follow that by taking a shiny instrument and peering into their ears. A friendly gesture would involve clasping them warmly by the wrist and peering intently at our watches. Doctors say they are taking our pulses when they do this, but what they are really doing is bonding with their patients.

One of the characteristics of a successful doctor is the ability to maintain a superior position. That is why doctors make their patients lie down on couches. It is much more difficult for the client to gain the upper hand from a prone position. They compound this by their choice of language. Instead of, as we are encouraged to do, gently probing to find out the source of the legal problem (which is often about an hour and a half away from the beginning of the first meeting with the client), doctors make it clear that they don't believe a word the clients is saying, by well designed questions like:

- "What *seems* to be the problem?"
- "How long *do you say* it has been going on?"
- "Does this hurt?" (usually accompanied by a firm jab in the ribs).

The *tour de force* of all medical treatment is the surgical operation. It is the bringing together of everything the medical profession has on offer: tubes, knives, gauze, instruments, squads of people in gowns, nurses, anaesthetists and surgeons. And what do we have as an equivalent?

The court hearing, of course. The gowns are black, not green, and the key performers wear wigs and not masks. But it could be said that the process is every bit as awesome. It is not for nothing that so often in trials a barrister is described as 'putting the knife in'.

From now onwards therefore trials are to be called 'operations' and the court room is to be sprayed with disinfectant before the proceedings start. And why not change a few other traditions. Counsel would look no more silly wearing facial masks than they do in their wigs. Time too for a change of colour. Black should give way to green, for gowns.

But back in the humble solicitor's office, the receptionist in her starched white dress and hat is addressing a client: "I'm sorry, Mr Smith does not do house calls, and his diary is booked fully until next week." Another client is shown out by a solicitor wearing a white coat. She looks very happy, for in her hand she clutching a document which says, in copperplate style: "Prescription".

Chapter 13:
Beyond belief

Originally published 8 December 2000

Whenever I ponder the American elections I find myself thinking of God. It is not that I am religious, or ready to pray for the candidates. I am not, and I am not. But the characteristic about that great and enigmatic country is that religion is now far more all-embracing than it is here. That was not always the case. In the Middle Ages, religion was everything here – a more potent force than the rule of law; but not any longer.

Many times have I been caught out when sitting down for an ordinary family meal in the USA when, fork of spaghetti raised to mouth and first chomp about to be taken, I am nudged in the ribs as everyone but me has their heads bowed, while the grandfather of the family embarks on a form of grace that is as full as the average supermarket trolley.

Religion in the States is big business. Opulent churches, catering to numerous denominations adorn every suburb. Aided by bright neon lights they lure their congregations inside, as a candle attracts a moth. If you go to an American church (even without a fork of spaghetti in your mouth) you will find that the God inside has a very much more direct concern about your welfare than in the average church here.

Since we first started hunting and gathering in earnest, our gods have taken many guises, but essentially the principle is always the same: a form of deity which is held to be omnipotent and from whom we derive life itself.

Yet if a neutral court was asked to decide, beyond reasonable doubt or even on the balance of probability if God exists in any form, I suspect that none (apart from the odd eccentric Norfolk magistrates court) would deliver a positive verdict.

We have had many investigations of late into issues of importance: rail crashes, BSE, Kamlesh Bahl (oops – sorry Law Society for more salt in the wounds). Those Americans who want to sue God should first establish that there is something there to litigate against.

What they need is to prepare the case properly. So, using modern Woolfish techniques, here is my advice on how to set about proving the existence of God in court, with apologies to clinical negligence practitioners who may think that their name is being taken in vain.

First of all, you need all the records. They will be required from all sources. Inevitably they will be in poor condition and jumbled up when they arrive. It will be necessary to sort them, paginate them (using, for the sake of balance, various types of numerals and counting methods) and ensure that sets are complete. If they are Dead Sea scrolls, care should be taken to ensure that a good copy is made. Running them through an old-style fax machine might produce a continuous print out, but don't delegate this to the most junior member of staff. You know how testy courts become when half a page is missing.

Then you will need to consider whether a transcription is needed. Handwriting is notoriously bad, and you will need to understand the abbreviations:

- LBIP = Leaves buttons (instead of coin) in Plate
- WOAC = Worships only at Christmas.
- C_2H_5OH = Has a drinks problem.

As to evidence, what will be needed is a scientific, double blinded cross-over study into the effect of praying: if there is a God, then prayers will be answered more often than by chance. As with all well-run investigations there will have to be controls, who are confirmed atheists whose prayers will never therefore be answered. A main frame computer will have to be booked to analyse the results.

And finally there will need to be experts. Now, as we all know, the best experts are those who approach the matter with scepticism, but who are persuaded to change their view when they have been properly informed. Those intending to prove the existence of God will therefore need to call upon reformed atheists; and those arguing the other way will need to find lapsed believers.

Other technical problems will have to be resolved. Will it be a small claim (on the 'still small voice' principle)? Or do we go for multitrack to reflect the diversity of the issue? How long will the trial last? Until the day of judgment of course.

But the real problem, as I see it, is that if there is a God and He (or She) participates, who knows what tampering with the evidence will take place? We will never know whether the result is reliable. Perhaps therefore we should abandon such a complex project before it is begun. There is a much easier way to demonstrate the existence of a deity, at least in America.

To me it is abundantly clear that it has been decided from on high that neither candidate is suitable to become the President. Therefore the Almighty, by a little celestial tinkering with chads* and numbers, intends to ensure that the next four years are spent in an orgy of litigation as the Florida votes are endlessly recounted, discounted, miscounted, counted up, and counted down. More and more court applications will be made, until the entire legal system is gridlocked with election issues.

So let's end with a real test. Please God, make the next election in this country a draw, and provide us all with enough work to last us for five years.

*This article was published during the 2000 US presidential contest between George W Bush and Al Gore. It was a very close run and the outcome was to depend on who won the vote in Florida. Many issues arose over the method of recording votes using punched ballot cards. If the holes were not punched correctly, votes were not recorded and the resulting incomplete hole was called a 'chad'. The result of the entire presidential election was delayed until the matter was sorted out.

Chapter 14:
Eyes right

Originally published 11 May 2001

They did not have contact lenses in Biblical times, but when I first tried them as a newly qualified solicitor I soon learned to understand what was meant by motes and beams. Since the age of 4, I have had to struggle with metal, glass and plastic contraptions perched on my nose. "You have a lazy eye," they said. So my active eye was covered in thick plaster and my lazy eye was made to see, whether it wanted to or not.

In due course it was decided that my bad eye had reformed sufficiently to be allowed a little assistance, and on the strict understanding – backed by a detailed agreement that I would otherwise be deprived of Trebor Chews or Mars bars – that my lazy eye was to play a vital part in my seeing activities for the remainder of my life.

At the Elm and Emneth Infants' School under the stern eyes of Miss Jermy who ruled the little academy of learning with a rod of iron (caning was permitted those days), I was known – when Miss Jermy was not looking or hearing – as Four Eyes (when wearing glasses) or Cyclops (when sporting a patch). Indeed I also became No Eyes when, as part of the various Fenland initiation ceremonies, my glasses were removed and stamped on, leaving my world a fog of blur and smudge.

And so there followed a succession of spectacles – slowly evolving over the years from the horrendous National Health Service standard issue (which made everyone look like an owl) through some pink plastic things (clearly the NHS that year had had a surplus of pink plastic), and eventually to the dull adult glasses that all dull adult solicitors wear.

In the meantime, my lazy eye stuck to its agreement; and between them my eyes did a reasonable job of seeing me through life apart from the occasional lapse when I failed to notice "now" instead of "not" in a legal agreement and nearly but not quite rendered the firm liable for the entire assets of the Solicitors Indemnity Fund.

Next came the onset of a combination of failing near sight and memory. The optician could no longer make lenses which enabled me to see distances and do close up work. It was the time in life for reading glasses, and the need to carry around two pairs of spectacles.

But then I became interested in Dr Thomas Stuttaford. Let me swiftly explain that I did not want to idolise him or keep press cuttings of his writings in *The Times*. I did not even read much of what he had written. It was much simpler than that: I want to be able to peer over my glasses in the way he does in his photograph in the paper.

I have for a long time felt the need to put people in awe of me. I am the sort who waits at a crowded bar for most of the evening to be served, while the under age, the pensioners, the regulars and even one or two of the more articulate dogs, come and go with their daiquiris, Old Speckled Hens and Cointreau and colas. Just when the bell goes for closing time does the bar person notice me with a "Sorry mate, too late, come back tomorrow".

So I felt that if I could look more imperious and convey menace in my appearance, the world might pay more attention to me. I have ruled out growing a beard or moustache, or acquiring those boots with high platform heels.

To me the solution is to peer severely over my lenses. My problem was that my eyes are fairly useless without lenses in front of them. If I try to see over my glasses, I may take on the Stuttaford look, but I will have no idea who or what I am looking at.

My previous attempt to wear contact lenses had ended in failure. The lumps of plastic I was expected to poke into my eye each day caused me so much pain that I had to go around wearing dark glasses even on cloudy days. I soon abandoned the attempt.

"Is that really a lens?" I asked, as I fumbled with something with about the same substance and texture as a wet sweet wrapper.

"It most certainly is," said the patient lady who was trying to teach me not only how to put them into my eyes, but also more importantly how to remove them again. It is said that if you learn to drive over a certain age you need an extra driving lesson for every year of your life. The same could be said of wearing contacts. It seemed to take forever to get the hang of it, but I was driven by my idol. I had to acquire the Stuttaford look. And it paid off. Now I can pop the sweet wrappers in and out of my eyes as though I was born with them. They feel good too. Two weeks into the experience and I hardly know they are there. Now my eyes do not steam up in hot kitchens, and I can still see out when in the rain.

And now I am negotiating for some expensive looking half moon glasses. Then I will go to the pub and positively terrify the bartender into giving me a pint of very Old Peculiar before closing time.

Chapter 15:
The cat that came back from the dead

Originally published 22 June 2001

I gave Ivan to my wife for her birthday some years ago. She had been reading about Turkish Van cats – with white bodies and splodges of ginger and with characteristic ginger tails. They also have an un-catlike predilection for water. Coinciding with her discovery of this species of cat, an advertisement appeared in a local newspaper inviting offers to purchase *one Turkish Van Cat by the name of Ivan, low mileage, one careful owner, full MOT etc.*

Ivan arrived the following day. Within hours he had taken a swim in the pond and scooped all the water out of his drinking bowl. It was not long before he had established himself at the top of the pecking order, terrorising our two docile Labradors. If I walked the dogs Ivan would run ahead and hide in the undergrowth. He would then ambush the hapless canines until they became so traumatised that they took advice about bringing a claim for PDCD (Post Dogmatic Cat Disorder).

He would also, when he chose to, be the conventional cat, dismembering small rodents and distributing their entrails throughout the house, and defeathering plump pigeons which he somehow managed to squeeze through his cat flap.

Rather in the nature of a managing partner he was both feared and admired. He grabbed your legs in a miniature attempt at a rugby tackle if he wanted feeding. Yet he also found time to show restrained affection and would sit on the laps of the children as they struggled with their homework.

The news of the accident came while Kim was navigating me into Catford. Kim is an excellent solicitor but has never got around to learning to drive a car. She roams the countryside visiting clients, and can do wonders from Aberystwyth to Bingley with local buses and the incomprehensible railway timetable. She can get anywhere in the country by public transport with ease. But put her in a car as a passenger, give her a map and tell her to navigate and she is lost. Or, as it happened, we both were.

Accordingly in our attempts to find Catford we encountered the Millennium Dome (twice), the North Circular Road (several times from different directions), London City Airport, and the science fiction world of Docklands. Suddenly we were among shining curvaceous colourful buildings, every one of which spelled innovation and progress. Why on earth did the Prime Minister not allow himself to be filmed electioneering in front of this backdrop instead of permitting himself to be berated by all those unreasonable people outside shabby hospitals who were insisting on their critical medical treatment taking place before they died?

Many false dawns and culs de sac occurred before Kim suddenly shouted "There it is." She was pointing at a number 177 bus. "Follow that bus and we'll soon be there," she exhorted. We followed, stopping regularly to put down and pick up passengers, cheating a little with the bus lanes and eventually being delivered to downtown Catford.

It was then that the news came in: Ivan had been killed on the road. Would I please bury him when I got home? Bad news punches you in the stomach. The death of a cat is not something you shrug off as you would a broken plate or a dent in the car. I had a lump in the throat all the way home.

The cat was lying in a cardboard box in the garage, curled up and looking as though it was asleep. I lifted up its body, gave it a last hug and placed it carefully in the hole which I had dug. I watched for a long time for any movement before I began to replace the turf. As I stared, I fancied I saw a faint twitch of the fur; but that could not have been. The cat was cold and very still.

The wake followed with affectionate reminiscences of the cat we had once known, and tearful speculation about the mayhem he was already causing in cat heaven.

At the end of the evening I was putting the house to bed when my eye caught a flash of white on the window sill. The flash of white was making a loud meowing noise, of the kind made by a cat which has not eaten for an eternity.

I opened the window and in crept – Ivan – very much alive and very much wanting his supper. I have written before about our ghosts (see *Haunted by the Law*, page 28), but the cat which was now in my arms was far from spectral, and also far from dead.

The pining children agreed. This was not a late cat; reports of his death had indeed been exaggerated. While the jubilation continued and the astonished Ivan was hugged almost to death, I sneaked out to the grave. It was intact. If he had risen from the dead, Ivan had carefully covered his tracks.

So what had happened? The only natural explanation is that our neighbourhood has (or had) two Turkish Van cats. The cat which died was Ivan's double which just happened to be run over outside our house, and is now buried in our garden. Ivan is now treated as a celebrity, and it will not be long before the pilgrims start to arrive to pay homage to the cat which came back from the dead.

The supernatural explanation is that Ivan died last week and has come back very visibly to haunt us, no doubt with the ghosts of the furry and feathery creatures he dispatched in his terrestrial life. But if that is the explanation, surely he should have the decency to stop devouring cat food.

Chapter 16:
Body talk

Originally published 3 August 2001

Nobody spoke as learned counsel took his position behind his desk at the start of a client conference, and fumbled for some time before he located the thick bundle of papers tied up in pink ribbon. Seated in front of him expectantly was the client leaning forward on her chair, hands clasped to the arms as though if she let go for a moment she would be flung into orbit. Beside her was the trainee solicitor also perched anxiously on his chair, his Adam's apple bobbing up and down and his arms folded in a cross in front of his chest. Next to him was the medical expert, who at that moment was standing with one hand in his jacket pocket examining the barrister's outdated text books.

Leading counsel in the meantime cleared a sufficient space on his cluttered desk to enable him to put his feet up and to show to those in front of him that he was in charge, that it was his desk and that it was time that he had his shoes re-soled.

Not a word had been uttered, but the body language of the four players spoke volumes. In the far-off days when all communication between solicitors and their clients, their experts and everyone else was in writing, nobody bothered too much about body language (apart from what happened inside the office, but we will draw a discreet veil over that). Solicitors dealt in carefully crafted letters which often took several days to prepare.

I remember a prolonged exchange of correspondence with the solicitor for a bank which had had the effrontery to want to repossess my client's house. Slowly, by move and countermove, we inched towards resolving the matter but there were still problems which just could not be sorted out by letter. In my mind I had conjured up a picture of my opponent as being grey haired with a military moustache, and a scowl on his face. Eventually we met to conclude the deal, and I discovered that she was young, pleasant and totally lacking a moustache.

As more and more people become familiar with body language it is important for us all to know what we and others are saying when we are not speaking. Here, for the benefit of the new students, are some signs to look out for.

Shake it all about. I personally am not an expert hand shaker. I often miss the clues and end up leaving some poor soul with his arm flapping in the wind or, when my own outstretched arm is ignored, having rapidly to find an itch to scratch.

If you get it right it is apparently important to show your dominance. This means going in palm down, and forcing your shakee to come at you in the supplicant position (palm up). If you are forced to shake in this way, it can be countered by using both hands in the kind of warm embrace that politicians are so good at. Alternatively you can grasp the shaker's arm or shoulder and give them a friendly pat, especially if at that moment you pull them into your personal territory.

Hand gestures. We British are not as good at talking with our hands as our continental cousins who display an infinite repertoire of hand signals. Here our hands give away a lot. Hands clenched together may appear to be an indication of confidence, but research (you may have thought that researchers did useful things but they spend a lot of time looking at hands) indicates that this is a gesture of frustration. How many senior partners (or judges for that matter) have you watched steepling their hands? This is a clear indication that they are in charge – and are they also invoking divine intervention?

At a recent meeting I noticed that every single person (myself included) had their hands behind their heads. I was not aware that I or they were making any point, but the clear message, according to the same researchers, is that what we were all saying was "Maybe someday you will be as smart as I am".

Heads I win. Of course heads must be the ultimate fountain of non-verbal communication. A head down shows disapproval. But the head on one side shows interest. If you are giving a lecture the ultimate goal is to have your entire audience with their heads on one side. If I give a lecture I feel lucky if half the audience are actually facing the front.

Legs eleven. If you cross your legs, this indicates a defensive or nervous position, but if you sit with one leg casually placed on your knee that shows you are being argumentative or competitive. Next time you are in a group, watch who has their legs crossed and who does not. The chances are that those who know each other will have their legs uncrossed and their arms relaxed.

For solicitors the name of the game is to observe everyone else without giving anything away yourself. We should all practise adopting the totally neutral gestures that indicate that we are both superior to the rest of the world and are totally in control. What if this catches on and non-verbal gestures are taken to be spoken? Will the professional conduct rules have to be changed to make the use of misleading body language a disciplinary offence?

If so, suspect that one or two among us might resort to that famous non-verbal gesture first introduced by Winston Churchill, and then slightly modified by a disenchanted horseman, involving the deployment of two fingers in the vertical axis.

Chapter 17:
Granny bashing in the blue lagoon

Originally published 15 February 2002

There was a thick fog of steam above the water. Beyond the lagoon, the sharp rocks stretched away into the distance. The water was as hot as any bath. Our bodies boiled while our heads froze. We could hear the menacing rumble of the volcano hundreds of feet below ground which was providing the heat (and the sulphurous smell). We were in Iceland's famous Blue Lagoon.

The first I noticed of the grannies was when they barged in front of us at Norwich International Airport. I don't suppose you knew we had an international airport in Norfolk. For that matter you probably didn't know we had an airport at all. But you are wrong. Norfolk has not one but two international airports. The first one (in time at least) is Northrepps International Airport. You will not find it on any maps. We only stumbled across it by accident when we were out exploring on the coast and saw a number of aircraft apparently diving into a field. Northrepps International is a grass strip with a portacabin, and an international departures lounge which consists of a plastic seat.

Which brings me to that other airport. Or rather it brings us to a dark morning at the end of January. When I was scraping the remnants of what the cat had brought home on to a newspaper, I noticed on the corner a readers' offer to go to Iceland for the day from Norwich. Knowing that my wife had always wanted to visit the place, I suggested we might give it a try, especially as the date fell on her birthday.

"Why would I want to spend the day in a frozen food supermarket?", she replied in a tone suggesting our marriage could be at risk. When I could explain it was Iceland the country that was on offer, the cloud lifted and the matrimonial threat receded.

I had only been to Iceland (the country) once before when I was returning from the USA on my first ever flight. We were to change planes in Iceland, and complete the journey to London on a Douglas DC6B (a converted bomber). As we taxied to the end of the runway, the outer engine on my side started to belch blue smoke. The takeoff was aborted, and we returned to the rudimentary terminal to be fed Spam while the engineers tinkered with the aircraft in a July snow storm.

I imagined that the demand for a Norwich-Iceland trip would be so low that we could all have been fitted into a Douglas DC6B, but we found the airport crammed with hundreds of people waiting in their anoraks to be whisked to the frozen north.

The grannies, one big one flanked by two diminutive ones, had obviously done all this before. They were not constrained by politeness or hesitation. In the blink of an eye they had slid to the front of the queue, and were presenting passports and tickets. Later they were first to board the bus for the plane, and somehow they had managed to acquire the seats with the most leg-room (even though the two small ones could easily have been stowed in the luggage lockers).

It remained dark all the way to Iceland. As we descended we could just make out frozen rivers, and icebound beaches. After landing, we were released into a huge airport terminal which was completely empty apart from us. The sun was just beginning to rise at 10 am.

The south west tip of Iceland felt like a journey back in time – a long way back. The landscape is bleak and grey, with no vegetation, and volcanic rock as far as the eye can see. It was like being on the surface of the moon. Plumes of steam erupted from the ground. Occasionally the flat horizon was interrupted by a fish processing plant.

Our first stop was the ocean, where we watched waves so cold that they left icicles on the rocks as they broke. Frozen to the marrow, we were then taken back across the lunar landscape to the Blue Lagoon. It was well organised. Towels, bathing costumes and luxurious robes were available to encourage you to go the short sub-zero distance from the building to the lagoon. We swam among the pumice stones and craters, while a throaty roar continued beneath us. It felt good. It also felt a long way from home.

As we emerged from the lagoon, I saw one of the grannies making off with my towel. It took a rugby tackle to prevent her escaping with it... Actually, she did no such thing, but I was almost expecting it.

Back in the bus (grannies got there first) we headed to Reykjavik, where I nearly precipitated further matrimonial difficulties by inspecting a well-known international fast food restaurant. I am pleased to report, Mr McDonald, that it was one of the cleanest and pleasantest of your outlets I have ever visited.

The town too was spotlessly manicured, with nothing out of place, and all life miniaturised. The Parliament has only 64 seats, and the Prime

Minister's residence was so small that an estate agent might describe it as bijou. We were told that you are likely to meet Iceland's famous in the streets, but we saw neither Bjork nor Magnus Magnusson. Maybe they had been chased away by the grannies.

Then it was back to the bus, and the journey back to the airport past frozen waterfalls and children in their hundreds skating on frozen lakes, with the sun setting behind the distant mountains – then home. And supermarket shopping the next day, but not perhaps in Iceland.

Chapter 18:
Sod's law and other disruptions

Originally published 2 November 2002

We are beset with laws. Why wouldn't we be? We are lawyers for heaven's sake. But in our keenness to familiarise ourselves with the laws and regulations currently in force such as *The A58 Trunk Road (Halifax to M62 Motorway Chain Bar) (Detrunking) Order 2002*, *The Merger Report (Interbrew SA and Bass PLC) (Interim Provision) (Revocation) Order 2002*, and not forgetting of course *Gorchymyn Addysg (Y Cwricwlwm Cenedlaethol) (Y Trefniadau Asesu ar gyfer Cymraeg, Saesneg, Mathemateg a Gwyddoniaeth) (Cyfnod Allweddol 1) (Cymru) 2002*, we sometimes overlook those other laws which govern us and which are just as important in their application to life in a solicitors' office.

Generally these are the laws which conspire to thwart and disrupt us. So let us return to law school and consider the real laws, starting inevitably with Murphy's Law.

Murphy's Law. Everybody knows this one: if a thing can go wrong, it will. It has a peculiar application to clients, usually those you bust a gut for and who seldom appreciate your efforts. If it is decreed by some superior power that a particular client shall be Murphied, then nothing will ever go right for that case. The file will vanish when the client arrives for an appointment in the office (only to reappear 20 minutes after you have struggled through the interview with only a shadowy idea of what you were talking about). Diary notes of key dates will be erased mysteriously. When you get to court you will turn up on the wrong day, and find that you should have been there a week earlier.

When you eventually win the case you pay the client too much and have to write begging letters to try to get it back. Then when you are sued for negligence all the careful attendance notes which should be on the file to exonerate you will be nowhere to be seen.

If you find you have a Murphied client, cut your losses, and immediately transfer the file to your worst enemy in the legal profession.

Coles Law. A salad consisting of cabbage soused in salad cream with a few raisins sprinkled on it. It has a rubbery taste and texture, and I would break this law any day.

Basset Law. A town in Nottinghamshire with a population of about 107,701 people, and I don't know any of them. But their MP John Mann does. He started his new year message this year: "Hands up if you think solicitors rip you off", and has been campaigning against inept solicitors ever since. So Basset Law, roughly interpreted, means that those who let their clients down had better watch out.

The Law of the Call of Nature. However much you need an adrenaline rush you should never have more than one cup of coffee (and never ever take a laxative) before appearing in court. There is no concept known to the law as 'Please sir, may I be excused'. If the court does not need to pee, nor can you. However it does explain why counsel, almost invariably, as the hands of the clock creep up to one o'clock, asks the judge "Is this a convenient moment, my Lord?".

The Law of Gravity. This important law is frequently ignored by solicitors, especially those who have not yet had a tongue lashing from a judge over some flippant remark which slipped into the inter partes correspondence. Most of us have, at some time in our lives lowered (or even raised) ourselves to correspond in rhyming couplets, or have permitted levity to creep into otherwise grave exchanges. The sad fact is that courts should be presumed to have no sense of humour and the moral is:

> If you get the urge to deal in wit,
> Sure as hell better stifle it
> For if you fail to treat with gravity
> The court will gaol you for depravity.

Poor Law. The law practised by those who deal in publicly funded cases.

Barr's Law. This law states that machines are as idiosyncratic as humans, which is not surprising, bearing in mind that they are made by humans. We have all experienced office machinery that misbehaves. How many have physically assaulted a jammed photocopier, or punched their computers in the solar plexus? But it is not just the office that harbours miscreant machinery. Try televisions and cars for instance:

> **The silly satellite.** We recently had a problem at home with our satellite dish. The engineers came out. They said there was nothing wrong. The problem remained, and we had them out again but

whatever the engineers did made no difference. The solution, discovered by accident, was to spray the satellite dish with water from the garden hose. This restores the whole system to excellent working order for several days. We later reported this discovery to the man from the television company. Far from praising us for a valuable discovery, they now seem to be avoiding us.

The crummy car. I have a car which runs on diesel. It also claims to be turbocharged, which means that it gets from 0-60 in three days instead of five. It has recently developed a fault: whenever I leave Norfolk, the turbo fails, and I find myself chugging alongside 40-ton lorries with no hope of overtaking. But try telling that to the garage. You immediately get that self-indulgent look reserved by garage proprietors for women drivers which says: "You don't know what you're talking about, you silly little man".

So having ventured briefly into alien laws, let us return to something more familiar. Let's see. This looks good: *The Road Traffic (Permitted Parking Area and Special Parking Area) (County of Norfolk) (City of Norwich) Order 2002.* I shall settle down for a rattling good read.

Chapter 19:
A ketchup week

Originally published 27 March 2003

The ketchup was the final straw at the end of 'that week'. 'That week' was one of the hardest of my life. Not because of the demands of case work, nor because of the male menopause, nor even because the managing partner was laying down the law. It was much closer to home than that. Others have Greengage Summers or Halcyon Days. Mine was a ketchup week.

It began when I waved goodbye to my wife at the crack of dawn and she sped off to the USA to torment some of our experts (we are involved in a rather big case. Someday I will tell you about it. Not now).

It is said that men are not very good at multi tasking. My wife says it. She makes me watch television programmes where they put men and women side by side with ironing boards, sinks full of dirty dishes, untidy bedrooms and bathrooms that have not seen a loo brush in months. Then they make the telephone ring, the milkman arrive, the rain soak the washing on the line and several children injure themselves simultaneously. It turns out that the women consistently outsmart the men both in terms of speed and effectiveness.

Even so, I had always thought that I was among the leaders of multi-taskers. It was not the physical things. I can turn my hand to ironing and make any shirt look crumpled. I can open a tin of baked beans and put a slice of bread in the toaster as well as any man, effortlessly delivering to a hungry mouth burnt toast and cold beans. I can even mix coloured and pale clothes before they go into the washing machine so that they emerge all looking a dusky grey.

The challenge was to co-ordinate everything so that it happened at the right time, like prodding two able-bodied teenagers out of bed, making sure that they looked vaguely respectable, stringing their school bags round their necks and getting them ready to leave punctually for school, while helping another teenager (who has some disabilities) to get into her clothes so that she did not end up with her shirt upside down or having missed breakfast.

Then I had to weave in the day job between the telephone calls from people trying to sell me double glazing or inviting me to borrow even more on my credit card.

Came 3pm and I was in full flow to a client. She was just getting to the point and expecting an intelligent response when I gasped that I had to dash to get the children from school. This is not what clients want, and the howl of outrage was still ringing in my ear as I churned the gravel in a futile effort to make up lost time. All the way along the winding Norfolk roads I was being taunted by my mobile phone. "Honest, officer, it was hands free all the way".

Scooped up the teenagers from underneath the wheels of the waiting school buses and drove them erratically home while still being menaced on my mobile. They were hungry, reluctant to do homework, keen to have friends round to stay, disagreeing on which television channel to watch and about what type of fast food I was to offer them that night.

And then there was the general mucking out, the washing up, the scraping of the thicker pieces of mud off the floor, feeding the menagerie (mainly animals, some children), making sure the house was not on fire before going to bed and then the whole thing starting all over again the next day.

There is a local Norfolk writer who in his weekly column makes regular reference to his offspring as Brat major and Brat minor. The same colourful description is given by some members of the Bar when they refer to their infant clients. Despite such endorsement, you will not find the word "brat" springing out of this page (at least no more than three times).

Because there is an upside of being a single parent too: the jokes and the conspiratorial and slightly wicked activities that we mice got up to while the cat was away, and the way that we all raced around trying to get some sort of order back into the place before she returned (we failed miserably).

But step fathers always fail somewhere, and when the supplies of tomato ketchup ran low the teenagers would not respond to reason. They made it clear that they would rather die than eat food bereft of it. They would not entertain the use of Brown or BBQ sauce. Fearing a rebellion, and the children phoning ChildLine or putting themselves into care, I set out into the countryside to search for supplies of the precious red fluid.

What I returned with silenced their criticism (and alarmed the local shops who feared that my purchases presaged a national shortage of the stuff). An hour later I staggered into the house laden down with 37 bottles of ketchup. Whatever else they complained of, it would not be a ketchup famine while I was in charge.

So let me end with a word to the wise: next time you act for a single parent who has not immediately responded to your letters, or filled in his or her child support forms correctly just think of what they are going through. And remember this too: if you squeeze a ketchup bottle hard enough it will form an effective weapon of mess distraction which could be used against you. But please don't ask how I know: now that I am no longer a single parent again my lips and ketchup bottle are both sealed.

Chapter 20:
How to stop a secretary crashing

Originally published 18 June 2004

Andrea, Ann, Betty, Elaine, Jane, Jennie, Jill, Karen, Liz, Maureen, Pam, Sally, Samanda, Stella, Sue, Vicky.

The list, to which must now be added Sue (again) Joan, Donna and Keri, reads like the women's section of a village war memorial.

These are the names of secretaries who, while not laying down their lives, nonetheless have had the misfortune over the years to listen to me rasping and spluttering in my dictation, changing my mind, refusing to take telephone calls, losing files, finding them in strange places, and generally wreaking mayhem as I have tried to grapple with this strange thing called the law.

It was predicted that with the advance of modern technology we would soon have the paperless office. That has not happened, and it may never happen because however clever and friendly computers become, nothing beats a sheaf of papers through which you can thumb, and on which you can scribble. Besides, one firm of accountants has found that paper use increases by 40 per cent in offices where there is internet access.

Others have prophesied that technology will deliver us into a secretary-less environment. If a computer can listen to you and turn the pearls of your wisdom into words that are correctly spelt, where is the need for any of the people on my roll of honour? Can we not do away with them altogether?

I think not, nor would I want to. The answer might lie in one of those horrible buzz words: *added value*. Secretaries do not just type. Gone are the days when whole rooms were filled with muscular women pounding away on their Remingtons and Smith Coronas, causing foundations to shake and setting up a cacophony which achieved a decibel level that nowadays would have caused health and safety officials to order the office to be closed.

Forgive me for dwelling just a little longer on muscular women. Not long after I qualified I ran a branch office with one secretary. We considered ourselves progressive, and we had an electric typewriter. When my secretary went on holiday her colleagues from the main office used to stand in for her, but they would not touch the electric typewriter for fear of shocks. Instead they would heave their huge manual machines out of the boots of their cars, then toss them down onto the desk with as much ease as the rest of us would take in moving a file (and a small one at that). In those days of course computers were still on the distant horizon. Now the things are everywhere – in cars, washing machines and even greetings cards. Yet it must never be forgotten that no computer can catch a fly – a task which is achieved with the greatest of ease by the common frog. Secretaries should take heart from this.

What computers will never do, for instance, is sort out difficult enclosures for letters, placate clients, arrange appointments or ask you if you really meant to say "you horrid little man" in your letter. And if they ever do we would probably resent them so much that we would want to smash their screens in.

But working with secretaries should always be a two-way thing – as indeed has been pointed out to me by the latest additions to my secretarial roll of honour. It's all to do with team work. If you treat computers badly, they will just crash but if on the other hand you work in harmony with your secretaries, between you so much more can be achieved. Sometimes the little things make all the difference.

So here, with a little help from my new friends, is a guide to the small things which can make a secretary very happy.

- If you dictate with files, place them face down as you finish each one. Magically the files will then be in the right order for typing when the pile is turned upside down. But remember not to spoil things by leaving the correspondence clip the wrong way round.

- Say on the tape when you have moved on to the next file, so that your secretary is not left to rifle fruitlessly through the paperwork in a vain search for the non-existent name of a correspondent.

- Try to dictate as though you are broadcasting. I dread playing back my tapes which seem to have an "er" or an "um" before every other word. It is also a kindness to spell unusual words – if you know how to; probably best to leave it to the secretary if you do not.

- Explain what you are doing. If you are trying to achieve a particular procedure, give an account of it. Your secretary will thank you for it, and more importantly will be able to help you get things right.

- Keep it interesting. Share your fascination for the case. Tell them the snippets [Mrs Gradgrind is the client from hell. Poor Mr Sprocket lost his fingers while bomb making in his youth, that sort of thing]. They have to hear you droning on for hours. At least give them some respite.

- Have regard for their despair. I used to show my virility by presenting my secretary with a pile of files a metre high accompanied by 4 tapes full to brimming with dense verbiage. Now, on instruction, I stop when I have reached the end of one side of the tape. In that way they can finish several tapes in a day – and go home with a sense of achievement.

Most importantly do not treat secretaries like computers, because if a secretary crashes you really will have a mess to clean up.

Chapter 21:
Death of a father

Originally published 28 January 2005

It was a cold January day. A small tearful group of us was huddled together. In the distance three horses looked on with mild curiosity before continuing to nibble at the grass. Nearer to hand the grave diggers were sitting in a 4x4 truck waiting for us to finish our task before they finished theirs. The congregation in the packed church murmured as they waited for us to return.

The vicar spoke the few sentences of the committal. The undertaker tapped twice with his stick, and at the signal the coffin was gently lowered into the ground. A few of us tossed flowers and some dry earth after the coffin. And then it was over: the end of a life, and the end of an era.

My father, David Barr, came to the Fens just after the war. He had just spent five years fighting the Germans, about which he was never keen to talk. He was the radio operator in a tank, but claimed that no one told him how to twiddle the dials, so his tank went in the opposite direction from the rest – which was just as well as all the others came under heavy fire while his was miles away, and safe. He nonetheless on another occasion was less lucky: the lid of his tank was hit and crashed on him, knocking him unconscious for ten days. He emerged with a tremor to his right hand that was to serve him well in his second great love in life: fishing.

Before he settled in Wisbech, he had a short spell as a judge advocate in Germany, where he stayed just long enough to organise for himself a blind date with a pretty young American doctor. With the confidence that only he could muster he sent her a note to say that she was about to meet the man who would be her husband. The ploy worked and they became engaged after 10 days and were married in three weeks.

So began the career of a man who drew huge admiration, and sometimes irritation too from all who knew him. Although he practised in what has become a bygone age of high street law, my father was never a conventional solicitor. He joined a drab, dingy office inhabited, so he said, by dragons male and female. He soon transformed it into an airy place with smiling staff.

While his colleagues were generating densely worded letters and cranking the handle of conveyancing, he was introducing new styles of letter writing, and creating comprehensible legal documents. He always said that a letter of more than a page was too long. His wills were brief almost to the point of fitting onto the back of an envelope. He prided himself in applying for probate, almost before the funeral had taken place.

He developed a taste for purple prose – but only in the sense that he wrote everything in purple felt pen; letters, formal documents, memos were all written or signed in this colour.

He hated pomp. He was a member of the Rotary Club for some years – but only to keep out his arch rival in the town. At one weekly lunch, members were invited to present something amusing. The rest came up with the standard array of safe jokes. My father insisted on playing to them "Be Prepared" by the American satirist Tom Lehrer. At the sound of the expression 'boy scouts' the fellow Rotarians smiled in benign approval as this smacked of the good works they all were familiar with. But when they heard –

"Be prepared! To hide that pack of cigarettes.
Don't make book if you cannot cover bets.
Keep those reefers hidden where you're sure that they will not be found,
And be careful not to smoke them when the scoutmaster's around,
For he only will insist that they be shared, be prepared!"

– they became apoplectic. I believe he never went to another meeting, but he had no regrets either.

His client care was legendary – even before the phrase had been coined. All his friends were his clients, and most of his clients were friends. Nothing was ever too much trouble. He would make them feel special. At the drop of a hat he would get into his Singer car (he had three of them in succession) and drive to the client's home. I was later to learn that there was sometimes an ulterior motive. He always carried his fly-fishing rod around in his car. The tremble given to him by his war wound was just the thing that, when transmitted to the end of a fishing line, convinced the trout that what was jiggling in front of them was a real insect. Inexplicably, many of the clients he visited most often lived not far from one of his favourite Norfolk chalk streams.

But even clients who did not further his angling career, were treated just as well, so that his became an impossible act to follow. His clients deemed the service they received from anyone else in the firm to be definitely second class.

Once he did go too far. "Take a letter," he said one day to his secretary (he never used a dictating machine in his life) "to that gorgeous young thing."

"Dear gorgeous young thing" began the letter – which was subsequently signed by another partner. Fortunately the gorgeous young thing took this new form of address in good part – and no doubt for ever afterwards expected more of the same.

He was undoubtedly eccentric but in a way that made people giggle helplessly. For most of his professional life he was the local coroner, and he conducted inquests in such a friendly way that those who suffered successive bereavements came to refer to him as "my coroner". Through the eccentricity there seeped a vein of immense kindness. He carried out little unsung acts of kindness throughout his life that people remembered years later and told about after he had died; a loan here, a bill payment holiday there, and a large unpublicised donation to a cause he supported. He loved raising money and would stage gala days to re-roof a church or get his favourite football club out of debt.

Well into his forties he sent an article on spec to a sporting magazine. To his delight it was accepted. For several decades he became a prolific author, publishing five books and more than 900 articles, including several dozen in *Solicitors Journal*. (Readers must blame him for setting my brother and me on the same path).

John Mortimer, the creator of Rumpole, wrote of his own father's death: "I'd been told of all the things you're meant to feel. Sudden freedom, growing up, the end of dependence, the step into the sunlight when no one is taller than you and you're in no one's shadow. I know what I felt. Lonely."

And that is exactly the way it feels. Lonely for the loss of a parent of course, but lonely also for a past age when being in the law was relevant to daily lives, when solicitors were usually general practitioners and cared for all their clients' needs from the first speeding offence to the last will.

Chapter 22:
Squirting and buzzing

Originally published 17 June 2005

The two sounds could not be more different. First there was the painful grinding of an elderly six-cylinder Bedford petrol engine, and then there was the soft soothing soporific hum, gentle and alluring, which could have been from a smooth-running electric motor, but here there was no electricity – at least none in the conventional sense.

In the first week of my summer break, my body clock remained finely tuned to my workaday life. For a year I had had five hours of daily commuting to work in Chelmsford. This meant the alarm going off at 6 am every day except Mondays, when it was 5 am because we had an early morning meeting.

Kirsten, my wife, described me in those first days as being like a coiled spring, tensing to be up and ready to grapple with whatever life threw at me; and to time record it down to the last second.

This summer was to be a time of catching up: dealing with the mounds of correspondence; mending the collapsed greenhouse; writing a book; decorating walls that have not felt the touch of a paintbrush for a decade; filling in my tax return before the last minute; and renewing close acquaintance with family and friends.

But it did not quite work out like that. I had no idea that life at home could be so busy. The telephone rings constantly. People turn up unexpectedly. Crises occur regularly. Running a home is a little like running a country without the civil service to help. The demands are continuous and unpredictable. You never know what will happen next. It could be two teenagers wanting lifts to opposite sides of the county at once, my daughter being rushed to hospital on the eve of her law finals or the tumble dryer developing such a penetrating squeak that all the bats in the area decide to decamp to Suffolk.

Days came and went with frightening speed. The piles of paper remained undiminished and the walls unpainted. But sleep came in huge boxfuls and the spring began to uncoil. Then things did begin to happen. We each had a catalyst and their noises ushered in the next phase.

I have been a frustrated fireman all my life. As a sad child I used to cycle furiously to the Wisbech fire station every time the siren sounded and then join the other little boys as we followed the lumbering appliance through the Fenland streets. As often as not it would be a false alarm or a chimney fire. But just every now and then a straw stack or a garden shed would cause the firemen to pull out their big hoses, connect up to hydrants and commit an impressive array of ladders and other gear – not to mention water – to the inferno.

Even now in middle age my pulse quickens if I see a bright red fire engine with blaring siren and flashing lights. Psychologists will no doubt identify some dysfunction in my make up and point to a severe case of fire engine-itis.

A few weeks before our summer recess, Kirsten rang me at work, with that tense sound in her voice that signifies a disaster of at least guinea pig death proportions.

The guinea pigs were alive and well but as she got up that morning her eye was caught by an item on television about the Ministry of Defence releasing 40 Green Goddess fire engines for sale.

"Don't be cross," she blurted, "I have just bought us a fire engine." Her initial aim had been to hide it, but even in my sleep deprived state I would have noticed a seven-ton fire engine parked in the drive. She had to own up.

And so to the other catalyst. For Christmas Kirsten did not want perfume or a book; all she wanted was a beehive. She had been fascinated by the little creatures all her life.

They both arrived at about the same time. The 49-year-old fire engine, complete with ladders, axes, bolt cutters, nearly a mile of hose and every conceivable way of sucking and squirting water, was delivered on a low loader. The beehive and accompanying equipment came in numerous boxes. For several weeks, neither stirred. Only one bee occupied the hive (and that was one that Kirsten caught trying to pump nectar from a paper flower – not perhaps the brightest bee in the bunch), and the fire engine stayed put because I found the forms to license it too difficult to fill in (I am only a solicitor, after all).

Gradually I recovered from the urge to pulse through my day at six-minute intervals. And the domestic demands began to let up a little. With a little help from a nice lady at the local DVLA office I managed to get a tax disc for the fire engine (zero tax and insurance £78 per year). At the same time Kirsten had a telephone call from the delightfully named Applebee Apiary to say that her humming box of bees was ready to collect.

Now she dresses up in a smart white bee suit and visits her new friends as they busy themselves building their colony and inspecting our garden.

And in another part of the garden I spend my days in an old Parisian fire chief's helmet working with a grease gun underneath the Green Goddess, or running out hoses and drenching the roof, the dogs and the postman.

When our long days are over, the conversation is no longer about the frustrations of the Civil Procedure Rules or the misbehaviour of a trenchant circuit judge. I now pour forth on the topic of hydrants, male and female couplings, featherweight pumps and hundreds of yards of hose while she drones on about brood frames, smokers, supers, queen excluders and even queens.

Chapter 23:
Still waters paddle deep

Originally published 12 August 2005

I did not expect deep thoughts to flow from the dogs' paddling pool, but flow they did. We had to buy the pool. Our dogs are aquatic creatures. One is a Newfoundland who dreams of rescuing sailors from sinking ships and the other is a brown Labrador whose greatest pleasure in life is in diving for his rubber ball. They both live for the moment when they can creep up unannounced and shake about 30 gallons of water all over us.

They used to derive their pleasure from a rancid revolting pond in the garden. The black murky water was reputed to be of a depth comparable to Loch Ness and to harbour creatures at least as ancient as Nessie. It was also a hazard to health and safety, with mosquitoes breeding there in their millions in the summer months.

So, a decision was made by the powers that be – my wife – that the pond should be filled in and replaced by something shallower, more manageable and not inhabited by creatures from the deep. The problem for the dogs was that while the new pond was being created, they had nowhere to practise their dog paddle or to provide the wherewithal to drench us.

Norfolk has a number of bargain stores that are my sanctuary when times are difficult. Mindful of the dogs' predicament I managed to procure for under £40 a gigantic paddling pool. The pool itself is covered with warnings printed in several languages telling you what you should and should not do with it. All, understandably, say that the pool should be used "under competent supervision" but it then becomes a testament to the cultural differences between nations.

Under 'GB' the warning adds: *Not suitable for children under 36 months. Contains small parts.* (Although the pool, as far as I could see, had just one part and would be difficult for a toddler to eat).

The Australians clearly need to shout: their warning is in print twice as large as the rest and tells users to consult their local council as fencing laws affect the pool, and not to leave young children unattended.

The US warning says: *Never allow diving into this product. Never place pool in another body of water. Guard against slips and falls in the pool. Follow these rules to avoid drowning, paralysis or other serious injury.*

As these three countries all speak roughly the same language, the warnings should be the same for all. Perhaps the differences are a reflection on lawyers in the respective countries. On the basis of the warnings, Australia is the least litigious and the US the most, with England somewhere in the middle.

At this point let me introduce Dr Frank Vertosick, a US neurosurgeon and author of an engaging book of neurosurgical reminiscence entitled *When the Air Hits Your Brain*. He is not a fan of ours, blaming lawyers for altering the practice of medicine.

Vertosick uses the real-life example of neurosurgeons treating a pregnant patient with a brain tumour: should they give her radiotherapy now, insist on a therapeutic abortion, or wait till the baby was born and risk the treatment being too late? "The radiation risk to the foetus derived as much from the fear of litigation as from tumour biology. Because a foetus is a blank slate, almost any jury award can be conjured up for a pregnancy gone bad. The unborn child represented a financial burden no one wished to bear," he said.

The upshot was that the foetus was not aborted. Radiotherapy was delayed until after birth – and the mother died. Dr Vertosick clearly thought that the outcome would have been different if it were not for the smouldering possibility of legal proceedings.

For most of my career I have been a claimant lawyer and have brought many claims against medical professionals. Vertosick's book should be compulsory reading for all of us in this line of work, because he gives us pause: he is candid to the point of poignancy about the things that went wrong in his professional career. He underlines that none of us is invulnerable (I have been sued for professional negligence twice in my career).

In some way, it is a pity that we are stuck with an adversarial system in this country. Sometimes everyone benefits from a little insight into what the opposition is going through. Not every medical accident is the result of culpable negligence. Not every injured client is a grasping greedy seeker of damages, as most defending lawyers would prefer to portray them.

Short of a fully fledged no fault compensation scheme, which is never going to happen, there will always be those who sue and those who are sued. But rights can be preserved on both sides of the litigation fence even if we are sensitive to our opponents' feelings. You cannot sue and be friendly, but you can acknowledge that most of the people who become caught up in the litigation machine are ordinary human beings doing their best in a difficult world. Some would say that the only exceptions are the lawyers – and their dogs.

So, back to the pool: I have arranged for both dogs to sign disclaimers, so that if they do suffer head injury while diving for their ball or pretending to rescue imagined mariners they will not sue me or the manufacturer of the pool in any English-speaking country.

That will not of course prevent them bringing a claim in some other jurisdiction, but as they are not rottweilers or dachshunds they might have difficulty with the language.

Chapter 24:
The savage poodle

Originally published 21 October 2005

It was, I suppose, the poodle that marked the end and the beginning.

The end had to come. For the previous 35 years I had taken my breaks from work in 14-day bites, and sometimes not even that, and seldom my annual entitlement. Last May I gave myself a four-month career break. At the beginning, the weeks stretched over the distant horizon. At first, the days went by quite slowly. Then, suddenly, the weeks raced by and far too soon it was all over without me achieving half the things on the list I prepared in the first week.

The night before the end, I behaved and felt like a pupil being sent to a new school. I prepared and laid out my clothes, chasing away the moths that had taken up residence in my suit, found a pair of socks that matched, and polished my shoes again. Then I had to get my satchel – otherwise known as a briefcase, find some pens that worked and locate my brain, which had been behaving like a piece of cauliflower all summer.

It was grim waking up in the half-light and rejoining the line of hapless commuters queuing to fight their way to their desks. As I neared my destination, the moths from my suit turned to butterflies in my stomach and a feeling of sheer terror welled up inside me. What would it be like now? Would I be welcomed or spurned? Would I know anyone now?

Seven and a half years ago I departed the comfortable environs of the firm I had been with for more than 25 years to try to give a fighting chance to a number of high-profile cases that had landed at my door. Then I was within six months of becoming the senior partner. At the time I wrote nostalgically about the people I had said goodbye to (see *Goodbye Norfolk*, page 19).

And after that lingering backward glance I embarked on a legal Odyssey that saw more adventure, more misery, more stress and more ridiculously long working hours than I care to recall as I worked my way through three firms of solicitors. I did not encounter the Cyclops, was not turned into a swine, but did manage to negotiate Scylla and Charybdis many times, and every day I felt like Sisyphus endlessly pushing a boulder up hill, only for it to be down at the bottom again ready for the start of the next day.

Yet despite all that, it has been a valuable learning experience. I have acquired, at first hand, knowledge of the inner workings of three very different establishments. It is a pity such encounters do not attract CPD points. If they did, I would never want for more CPD hours in my life.

If someone were to thrust a microphone into my face and ask me what the take home message was from my Odyssey, I would answer:

- The best run firm is the one where the management has the confidence of the staff and vice versa. If your staff are miserable and demotivated you will automatically lose at least 25 per cent of output. If you trust your staff you will, generally, find that that trust is repaid with considerable interest.

- Time is more important than money. Almost everyone would prefer to have flexible working hours than even quite a substantial pay rise.

- If you are going to reward your staff, then do it properly. If you plan to dish out a mouse mat for Christmas, or a chocolate egg at Easter, then save your effort. You will cause more resentment than if you had done nothing at all. Far better to take them greyhound racing or to Amsterdam for the day (been there and got both tee shirts).

- Treat emails as a menace rather than a boon. In one of the firms, I had to spend about an hour a day simply reading my emails, many of which were internal. At the other extreme, another firm denied all direct internet access to its staff. If you wanted to send an email or search the web, you had to get permission first and go to a workstation at the far end of the office under the watchful gaze of busts of the founding partners. Emails are dangerous. In one firm there were some lively internal exchanges about a truly dreadful client who would give no one any peace. The comments about the client became less and less restrained. Inevitably, someone then pressed the wrong button and the entire dialogue was then dispatched through the ether – to the client. All in all I prefer the 'no emails' approach. It is safer, and a sight more peaceful.

- Barristers are not gods, and nor are eminent experts.

Life has now gone in a complete circle. Last week I returned to my old firm, and there they all were as though nothing had changed. True there were one or two additional grey hairs and a couple of extra wrinkles, but it was the same cast, ready for further adventures – vegetarian, Jamaican, and G&T. The only missing one was my bearded partner. He was there large as life, but of his beard there was no sign, so in due course he will have to be rebranded.

So it's been a long journey from A… to A. I knew I had come home when, on my first day, I was asked to see a client who had been savaged by a poodle. The pugnacious pooch had clamped its jaw over the client's ankle, and bitten it so hard that the client had to have emergency surgery. Now that's the kind of case I understand.

Chapter 25:
Apples from Wisbech

Originally published 16 December 2005

The time was last Saturday, but it was not just last Saturday. It was a substantial part of the last 20 years. Time, according to scientists, is not a linear thing. It is more, so they say, like pressing a large piece of elastic material. It bends and twists. In theory it goes back as well as forward – and that is a little how it felt when a small group of us went to a remote part of the town for the firm's annual Christmas outing.

It was not the normal kind of outing, with spectacular entertainment, good company, strong drink and gourmet food. Nonetheless what had to be done had to be done, and traditionally, Christmas time was chosen as the moment to do it.

The managing partner turned a large key and pushed open a small door which creaked menacingly on its hinges. We were let into a large cold warehouse. High above us bare light bulbs cast strong shadows on the long rows of shelves draped with cobwebs. Between the rows were boxes, marked "Apples direct from Wisbech". On the concrete floor lay piles of yellow, green, red and blue files. Something scuttled away into a corner.

We were gathered together in an orgy of destruction. Office files dating back two decades had been heaped together in their apple boxes for us to sift through before they were recycled into toilet paper.

Our task was to go through them one last time to make sure that they did not contain any dark secrets or valuable documents. In doing so we were transported back in time to a different era. Here was a time capsule bearing the now withered fruits of energetic endeavours. Many of us were generalists then, dealing surprisingly competently with whatever the clients threw at us – wills, divorce, trips to the magistrates' courts, house buying and selling. We had not learnt then to say "that is outside my area of expertise" or "you must see our criminal department about that." It was an age of innocence: if a client wanted it done, we did it – even if the client wanted us to arrest a ship (as one file revealed), and we had absolutely no idea how to do it. We operated on a wing and a prayer and mostly avoided disaster.

There were names from long ago that brought back memories – the roguish brothers who spent much time lecturing us on the need to be absolutely scrupulous in business, but then they were both sent to prison for defrauding Customs and Excise; or the most miserable builder who ever darkened East Anglia. Twenty five years on he remained miserable but has in the meantime become a millionaire, while those of us who served him will have to work into our seventies to avoid running out of pension. His file concerned a cow in his expensive swimming pool. And there were thick files all about raging disputes between neighbours, bulging with our careful efforts to quell the flames of dispute.

We noted sadly that many of the beneficiaries of our efforts were now dead as were even some of our colleagues whose handwriting was preserved in those files.

What was remarkable was the almost complete absence of standard letters. In most cases there was not a client care letter to be seen. Correspondence, mostly typed manually (usually only the carbon copy on flimsy yellow paper was on the file), was short, seldom going over into the second sheet. But as you thumbed through the pages, a much more personal feeling emerged.

We attended to other detail then too: many documents were sewn along the edge, and contained neat lining off of sentences and paragraphs. Despite the chill of the surroundings, a real warmth radiated from the files.

When we come to destroy our current cases in the decade after next, the picture will be very different. We will see much longer letters to clients, advising them in impersonal terms of every single aspect of their transactions, whether they like it or not. We overload our clients with information about how to complain about us, how to challenge our bills, how we do or do not advise them on financial services, and how we are obliged to grass on them if they but whisper that once, a very long time ago, they paid their cleaning lady cash in hand and did not account for the PAYE. Because we have to say so much the clients have to search hard in the dense overgrowth of our verbiage for something that is really about them and their case.

The documents in our files are plain, confined to piles of A4 paper, colourless creations without character and totally forgettable. There is no handwriting in the files, except the weary signatures of clients who have been obliged to give us authority for every faltering step we take in their cases, and every time we sneeze or go to the loo.

The chill Christmas outing in 2025 will not be thawed by the warmth from the content of the files.

Will there be a backlash? Might we in years to come describe a complete circle? Clients are encouraged to believe that solicitors should be as easy to instruct as it is to buy baked beans or Andrex. Those in our profession are often spoken of as "ambulance chasers". Mud sticks, and government spokesmen and their spin doctors have found that if you repeat a label or tag often enough the idea takes hold – like the myth of the compensation culture which is perpetuated even though it does not exist.

For future presents to our clients, the Law Society should produce the Book of Care. This turgid volume will contain every facet of client care, political correctness and regulatory compliance that anyone can dream of, and be available in many formats – video, audio book, dramatised on the London stage. Bound in genuine calfskin, it will look so good that no client will ever be tempted to read it. Having painlessly complied with whatever we are required to do, we can let our files once again focus on the rolled-up-sleeves law that we were trained to practise. Jokes and personal notes can creep back between the pages. Legal documents will again be adorned with ribbons and seals. Better still, we will be able to charge sensible fees. Visits to the warehouse at Christmas will be fun, the public will love their solicitors again, and Christmas puddings will be thrown at any politician who dares to say otherwise.

Happy Christmas!

Chapter 26:
Smallbone alive

Originally published 3 March 2006

"This is just like the setting for *Smallbone Deceased*." My comment drew frowns of bewilderment from those who were giving me the guided tour.

It was my first visit. Earlier I had driven across the flat landscape that characterises the 400 square miles of land making up the Fens. The Fens – for those who have not yet included it in their life's itinerary – is an area that used to be largely under water, where villages were often cut off from one another in the winter months and whose inhabitants are reputed to have webbed feet.

Our firm now has three offices, enclosing in a large triangle about a tenth of the area of the Fens. It is not the Bermuda Triangle, but it is nonetheless easy to disappear without trace in the featureless landscape of loamy settlements with names like Wormegay, Friday Bridge, Black Ditch Level and of course Six Mile Bottom.

At the southernmost tip of our triangle lies the sleepy town of Downham Market. A few years ago we took over the office there of the only sizeable firm of solicitors.

Much has been done to the office since then. Computers have replaced manual typewriters, threadbare carpets have been torn out and have given way to our firm's shade of blue, and the heating system now works for quite a lot of the time.

But what has not changed is the all-pervasive atmosphere of a traditional solicitors' office. Cupboards are stuffed with old ledgers, and several large outhouses have floor to ceiling shelves with neat little boxes containing the work output of several decades.

Nor has there been any change in the problems thrown at us by the public we serve. While I was there an elderly dog arrived, complete with its bowl, a packet of biscuits and a small toy. It was an unwanted bequest. The beneficiary had decided to decline the substantial sum of money offered for its upkeep and had returned the dog, its worldly possessions and the cheque to the office.

The *pièce de résistance* is the strong room. It leads off from the reception area and is huge. Thousands of sets of title deeds, all neatly indexed, line the shelves. They exude a particular musty smell that is the exclusive olfactory preserve of solicitors' offices.

And below the shelves were the deed boxes, several of them each large enough to contain a body.

Last month saw the death, at the age of 93, of Michael Gilbert. He was a solicitor and a prolific novelist. He was also the author of one of my three favourite novels about the law: *Smallbone Deceased* – the other two being Harper Lee's *To Kill a Mockingbird* and *The Franchise Affair* by Josephine Tey.

Smallbone Deceased is a delicious whodunit set in a solicitors' office at a time before electronic gizmos. When the body of a trustee is found in a deed box, everyone becomes a suspect. Every chapter title is a legal expression – starting with *Parties to the Deed* and ending with *The Bill of costs is presented*, pausing along the way to cover *Preliminary enquiries*, *Discovery of a Document* and *A very puisne mortgage*. It is every bit as gripping as an Agatha Christie novel and contains many twists before the plot unravels.

I don't expect that our Downham Market strongroom contains any dead bodies but as I glanced across to the huge Tesco store glowering on the opposite side of the road I wondered where this office and many other similar offices up and down the land will be in ten or twenty years' time.

The public is not good at supporting solicitors. In opinion polls we come only just above politicians. Curiously if those who have actually used a solicitor are asked, our rating shoots up. We are not as cuddly as nurses or admired as firemen or worshipped as the cast of *Eastenders*. Whenever our bad apples turn rotten, it makes news headlines. Yet whenever we give our time for nothing or fight well beyond the call of duty or at the miserable rates of pay given in some areas of endeavour by legal aid – no one hears about it.

We will never have the commercial clout to change public perception by media campaigns. A television drama about nice solicitors would soon have viewers switching channels. But what we can do to compete with Tesco law is to keep offering that special human contact that distinguishes us from others. If you go to a doctor you get, if you are lucky, an eight-minute slot. If you try to contact a government department you will be fortunate to speak to a human being after a morning of trying to get through on the telephone. And I do not need to mention call centres with the endless requirements to press buttons before you can get to listen to Vivaldi's *Four Seasons*.

We need to sell the old-fashioned values of personal service and time to listen, combining it invisibly with all the efficiency that technology can offer us. If clients can get back to knowing that with their solicitor they can develop a relationship with someone they can trust to guide them in all their legal encounters through life, we can surely see off those whose exclusive aim is to make a fast buck by offering the simplest legal services off aisle 21.

But we must watch it. If we do find dead bodies in our deed boxes, that might not do our business a deal of good – though it would still be far more interesting to the general public than anything that happens in Tesco. And I wager that those who promote Tesco Law will not have the faintest idea how to cope with the contents of a deed box even if it does not contain a corpse.

Chapter 27:
Camel antics

Originally published 23 June 2006

It was so sudden. One minute I was walking along minding my own business, and the next minute there was this rumble then a crash followed by a thud followed by a painful blow to my head. If I had had a haircut, as I had been promising myself for weeks, I might have been felled by the blow, but my wiry hair acted as a shock absorber and I ended up more startled than injured.

Our family has a problem. We have a fundamental inability to throw anything away – ever. This is compounded by a terminal case of bibliophilia; our house is crammed with books. They spill out of shelves. They form a wall around every bed. They prop open doors and hold up shelves for more books. And they multiply.

That may explain why, on the night in question, several legal tomes that had been piled high on the top of a tall bookcase suddenly decided to make a break for freedom and propelled themselves onto my head as I walked past them.

One of the consequences of being a solicitor who loves books is that if well-meaning family or friends cannot think of anything else, they give me a long-forgotten treatise on the law in the expectation that I am bound to find it fascinating.

The books that assaulted me came into that very category. They had been gathering dust for many years because it is hard enough these days to find time to read a novel, and I am not yet so sad that I feel the urge to dive into *Legal Decisions Affecting Bankers Vol. IV 1924–1936*.

However, after that book had plunged towards my head it fell open at the report of the case of *Westminster Bank Ltd v Hilton*. It also opened a window into a bygone age – a dispute involving a cheque for £8 1s. 6d. For those of you who came into existence after 1970 that amounts to £8.07. The customer tried to stop his cheque by sending a telegram to the bank but gave the wrong cheque number. The bank paid the cheque then subsequently bounced another cheque for £7 after the customer was found to have only 3d (that's three old pence by the way – equivalent to one and a half pence now) in his account, and the customer sued for damages for negligence. The judge decided in favour of the bank. Then the Court of Appeal found against the bank, until the House of Lords exonerated it. And all over £7. No problems over proportionality in those days, with apparently no lack of enthusiasm for litigation.

Next to assault me was the *Modern Law Manual for Practitioners,* published 61 years ago to assist solicitors who had returned to practice after fighting in the Second World War. In a mere 650 pages the book set out to cover the entire law of England: "without some such aid a busy man cannot hope to bridge the gap of the war years".

Some of its comment applies just as much today as it did in 1945: "What is new is (i) the extent to which in recent time Parliament has made use of the device of delegating its powers, even in cases where major matters are involved, and (ii) the immense volume of delegated legislation which has accumulated in the last 50 years and which gives a new aspect to English law, and (iii) the practice of amending Acts by Orders".

I received a lighter blow (on my ear) from *A Lawyer's Notebook*. This little marbled volume first hit the public in 1932 (that is, before it hit me in 2006). According to its introduction the anonymous author lived the kind of life that solicitors only dream of these days. He left for work at 9.30 am and arrived at his office in Lincolns Inn by 10am. At two thirty he would go for lunch in the back room of an oyster shop in Chancery Lane where he drank "a light Moselle and a tawny port", returning to the office just in time to sign his post before leaving at 5.30 to go to a Turkish bath on his way home. This relaxed man kept a note book by his bed "in order to note forgotten engagements and useful meditations on his business". However he evidently could not resist allowing the entry of wider interests. The result is a delicious collection of thoughts and articles. Of jazz he said: "it suggests the antics of a camel copulating with an elephant". On indecent literature: "A dirty mind is a perpetual feast, and no policeman is going to destroy this priceless possession of the human imagination".

He had obviously also read an earlier volume of *Legal Decisions Affecting Bankers,* as he pointed out that we are in the last resort governed by banks, adding: "I should certainly far prefer to be governed by banks than any of the white-livered socialists who purport to lead any of the so-called parties in the House of Commons."

But his comments about bank managers could well hold good today: "I look on the modern bank manager as the kind of person who hands millions to a Hatry [a speculator who was thought responsible for precipitating the US economic depression of the thirties] and dishonours little cheques for £1."

And of lawyers he simply says: "the test of a good lawyer is to know what can be said or written yet even more what can neither be said nor written but merely understood."

And the lessons from this unexpected journey into the past? First, that things may not have changed as much as we thought and, second, beware falling law books: they could do your head in.

Chapter 28:
Holiday from hell

Originally published 18 August 2006

"And did you have a good holiday?"

"No, it was dreadful," I growled to the first person I met back at the office after it was all over. Never take children on holiday with you." From then onwards it was only my vegetarian partner, who himself had had rather a splendid holiday, who dared to raise the subject again.

It was a long time ago, a really long time ago. But I still remember my first French lesson. I was coached by a retired brigadier in the art of conjugating *Je suis, tu es, il est* until *les vaches* come home. I could not become enthusiastic for all those French expressions, and the pictures of quaint French towns with their men on *bicyclettes avec les oignons et les pains*. I had been steeped in the view that the French were garlic-eating, Gauloise-smoking, wine-drinking, regulation-flouting no goods; and that if ever one was to go to France it was purely for the purpose of passing through to gain access to a more worthwhile country.

Then I discovered the Channel tunnel and found to my surprise how easy it is to drive to France, even from Norfolk, and how much the French have improved since I went to school.

Last year we made two successful sorties into northern France and this summer we decided to make it the big one. Between us my wife and I can summon up six offspring, all of whom are now just about adult. Five of them decided to join us. Add to the pot a couple of 'partners' and a satellite navigation system, and there you had a recipe for disaster.

I will remember that holiday long after those rather dull affairs involving sun, sea, Spain and sangria. It is said that the chaos and disruption from your children increases according to the square of the numbers involved. The square of 7 yields a chaos factor of 49, and that was reckoning without the satnav. Fur and feathers flew. Sulks and rebelliousness abounded, and our satellite navigator was constantly trying to get us to drive across open fields or approach our destinations by forming several cartographic loops.

But secretly I found it much more enjoyable than I was prepared to say. The country – at least Normandy, which is as far as we ventured – seems to have retained a calm and sense of proportion that somehow we have lost in England.

It is all too easy to view a foreign country through rose tinted spectacles when you are taking your precious annual break, but remember that for us our spectacles were smeared and blood-spattered. Although many have commented on the joys of France the things we noticed and particularly liked were:

An absence of lawyers. There must have been lawyers but they were little in evidence – no advertisements to be seen in the papers, no garish offices. One of the French words for lawyers is 'avocats', which also means avocado pear. If 'solicitor' was also the name of a fruit what would it be? A lemon? An ugli fruit?

The roads and motorways. They were smooth, uncrowded and traffic cone-free. The service areas were frequent and inviting. True you had to pay tolls from time to time, but it was a small price to pay for such good roads.

The lack of plastic carrier bags. The supermarkets we visited just did not dish out carrier bags: you either had to buy them or do without. One did not even sell bags. You were directed to a store of old cardboard boxes. Marine species, which apparently mistake the bags for jellyfish and then die horrible deaths, are benefiting from this French 'take it or leave it' attitude. Ireland can manage without plastic carrier bags too, so why not the UK?

The lack of the 24/7 culture. France closes for lunch for two hours, and almost everything, supermarkets included, shuts down aside from the sidewalk cafés. Very little is open on Sundays, and I defy you to buy petrol in the evening if you are not French. There are a few automatic fuel stations, but they accept only debit cards issued in France. "Je regrette", the message seems to be, "Vous Johnny foreigners ne pouvez pas achêter l'essence ici, après dix-huit heures, parce que nous avons better things to do than hang around waiting to serve vous".

The language. I hated learning French, but it is so useful to be able to say more than "please", "thank you" and "may I have the bill". When a visitor arrived at the place where we were staying, and asked for directions to a nearby museum, I was able to tell him clearly how to find it. We conversed for several minutes in my best schoolboy French until the visitor eventually asked if I spoke any English. It turned out that we were both English. After that I was able to give him even better directions, and correct the fact that I had confused my *droite* with my *gauche*.

Above all, the bread. The village in England I was brought up in had its own bakery in the '60s, but there are now very few of them in England. In Normandy, almost every village or hamlet still has a bakery, enticing you every day with its scent of new-baked bread. And when you have tasted it you never want to go back again to mass produced English supermarket bread.

One of the delights of our visit was a trip to the Bayeux Tapestry, a low-tech video of the Battle of Hastings. The English are depicted in this and other medieval documents as long-haired, argumentative louts who can't hold their beer. Now surely they got that very wrong. Judging from our own offspring, nothing could be further from the truth. Or could it?

Chapter 29:
Roly Poly Stones

Originally published 22 September 2006

His whole body shuddered, as did the foundations of the Millennium Stadium, as he gyrated, punched the air and bellowed at the top of his voice. Beside him his two teenage children clearly wanted the ground to open and swallow him up, as well as themselves: their expressions spoke terminal embarrassment. But this stout solicitor was not to be fazed by such things. No teenagers were going to spoil this moment.

Earlier, I had spoken to him, as you do when you are sharing an unusual experience, such as traffic gridlock or a bank robbery. He was a conveyancing solicitor who had added a number of inches to his waist, and several kilograms of weight since he was a sixties pop fan. This occasion was now part of his secret life.

We all have secret lives. The archetypical secret life was enjoyed by Walter Mitty. For those who have not encountered him, Walter Mitty was invented by the US humorist James Thurber. Bullied by his wife, derided by passing members of the public, cowed by traffic police, Walter Mitty was in his imagination a fearless wartime leader, an expert surgeon, a magnificent lover and even a courtroom supremo. When he was in his secret world he was frequently accompanied by the sound of machinery, gunfire or engines that always went pocketa-pocketa-pocketa – until he was dragged back to reality by the outside world. There is a piece of Walter Mitty in all of us.

Nowadays studies have examined the secret life of anything from bees to trees, or moody cows to lobsters. Everything and everyone, it seems has a secret life. But do solicitors? Most of us greyly travel to our offices, greyly carry out our daily duties and then return home at the end of the day, grey and exhausted. It was refreshing therefore recently to find out, as part of an exercise to revamp our website, that some of those who work with me splash a little colour into their lives – including: racing antique sports cars, acting in amateur theatricals, preaching at a local church, running a bed and breakfast and part time nursing and playing rugby – this last being a female solicitor in her fifties who should know better.

One of the rarer aspects of my secret life consists in going to rock concerts. Rare because I have only done it twice and more than 40 years separated the two secret activities.

Cambridge. Nineteen sixty something.

The main event was still an hour away. We were on the edges of our seats. The warm up bands were playing, and we were listening politely to them. Then after an age, the curtain went up to four well kempt young men in smart suits, all with pudding bowl haircuts and all (but one) sporting guitars.

They were on for half an hour. The screaming started when the curtain rose, and did not abate until long after the curtain had fallen and they had left the theatre. No one could hear a single note they played.

The four young men were the Beatles, just before they reached the height of their popularity.

At the time, there was another popular rock band. In contrast with the Beatles, its members were rebellious and wild. Our parents tolerated the Beatles because they looked clean and wholesome, but they took against the Rolling Stones who, they felt, were a corrupting influence.

Last month. Cardiff. The Millennium Stadium.

There were so many of us travelling to Cardiff in our sensible estate cars that we caused traffic hold ups as far back as the Severn Bridge. Earlier there had been a move to reduce the number of tickets available to members of Saga, for fear of the entire audience consisting of senior citizens.

As we approached the Millennium Stadium, we could spot fellow concert goers. They were the ones who would have been teenagers in the '60s. Now, many had their own teenage offspring in tow, some looking distinctly unenthusiastic about what awaited them.

We filed into the stadium and obediently took our seats. The bouncers at the door eyed us suspiciously. Surely, they must have thought, they cannot all be well behaved. There was a warm up band. I cannot recall their name (though I can remember that prior to the Beatles we were treated to Freddie and the Dreamers and Marianne Faithfull among others).

We applauded them politely when their performance was over. Then there was a pause – presumably to enable us to buy overpriced beer and even more over priced Rolling Stones paraphernalia. It gave us an opportunity to get to know those who were near to us. Within a fifteen-foot radius I identified two other solicitors. There were twenty five thousand of us packed into the stadium, and it is therefore a safe bet that a not insignificant number of solicitors were in the audience. Were you one of them by any chance?

Then with an explosion of fireworks and twang of guitars they were there – our teenage idols and all nearly old enough to draw their pensions – Mick Jagger, Ronnie Wood, Keith Richards and Charlie Watts. To start with, we sat quietly through *Jumping Jack Flash*, *Oh No Not You Again*, and *Let's Spend the Night Together*, applauding in the same way that one would acknowledge an accomplished performance of a Beethoven quartet.

Then slowly, a metamorphosis came over the audience. Our hair lost its greyness and our behaviour grew wild. Polite applause became buried by loud shouting. We stood. We jumped. We climbed onto our chairs. We sang the words we knew so well and we punched the air to ram home the lyrics. And however lively and noisy we became, we were outdone at every turn by the stout solicitor who was having the time of his life – while Mick Jagger pranced and ran the length of the huge stage showing that old age does not have to be a handicap for anything, Keith Richards (who had lately fallen out of a palm tree) entertained the audience by being the only person in that huge auditorium to break the no-smoking rule, and hurling his dog ends at us.

Long before the end of the concert we were waving and yelling and stamping. The stout solicitor clearly knew all the words, which, according to reports, was more than Mick Jagger did as he apparently had to use an autocue. If he had sung "pocketa-pocketa-pocketa" to fill the gaps we would have forgiven him, as that is the sound that comforts all of us in our secret worlds.

The following day we returned to our desks. The greyness had, for the moment at least, been supplanted by the excitement of the previous night. I have no doubt that the stout solicitor still sings the complete words of *Satisfaction* to his colleagues at the beginning of each working day. And their response? Pocketa-pocketa-pocketa of course.

Chapter 30:
The smell of success

Originally published 26 January 2007

The news that a local DIY store made its job applicants dance to the Jackson Five song *Blame It On the Boogie* as part of their assessment caused something of a furore nationwide, but to those of us who practise in the county of Norfolk it comes as no surprise at all. Nor indeed did the fact that candidates were asked to pull funny faces that were then photographed by managers.

Norfolk is a county where PC still stands for what it started as – the man on the beat who chases after you if you raid birds' nests or rob Farmer Blair of his apples.

But if you do get your candidates to dance the hokey cokey or sing Elvis Presley's latest hit, how do you sort the good from the bad and ugly?

However superb the CV, you do in the end have to decide in the space of perhaps no more than half an hour whether the person sitting in front of you will not only perform well at the tasks you allocate to him or her, but also not put the backs up of your sensitive and intolerant staff and certainly not smell.

A few decades ago we had a secretary who was challenged in the armpit (malodour) division. Partners' meetings disposed rapidly of minor issues, such as whether the firm was making a profit, or how many of the partners had been struck off that month.

That enabled full attention to be given to the armpits of Miss Whiff, as she came to be known. She had already precipitated several mass walk-outs in the typing pool.

The problem was that Miss Whiff was a formidable character, who did not take kindly to suggestions even that a comma in her typing had been misplaced. If she made an error in a lease nobody had the courage to tell her so and it usually fell to the junior partner (who had once foolishly admitted that he could type) to spend the weekend laboriously retyping the 100-page lease of number 33 Acacia Avenue on one of the firm's giant Remington manual typewriters.

Various stratagems were adopted. The typing pool became like a florist shop, bursting with a glorious array of sweet scented flowers from all over the world. They were not a match for Miss Whiff's armpits. The plants rapidly withered under their onslaught.

Eventually Miss Whiff provided her own solution to the problem by quietly expiring while typing a particularly vitriolic letter before action. It was several days before the local undertakers could get near enough to retrieve the body.

In later years job interviews were conducted in the presence of a little Jack Russell owned by another partner. It had a way of raising one eyebrow if it detected any unpleasant smells, thus ensuring that from then onwards the typing pool remained fragrant and the flowers survived.

Olfactory issues aside, how do you pick the best candidate? Do you, as some firms do, pick only those with first class honours, then make them complete a series of psychometric tests? One firm I know of had a panel of interviewers each of whom were required to fire difficult questions at the candidate – machine gun style. One candidate grew tired of this version of the Spanish Inquisition and stormed out of the interview muttering that it was the strangest interview she had ever encountered. Personally I would have given her the job to reward her courage, but others felt that she would only be trouble.

So how do we, out in the sticks, perform the interview task? Over the weekend I joined in a reunion of old work colleagues, all of whom I had interviewed for their jobs. I asked them what it was like. One pointed out that I kept her waiting for 15 minutes. Another admitted that she had lied to me and that despite her confident sounding response she did not have a clue how to handle emails (I never did find out – by the time she started she was emailing like nobody's business). Another said that we spent the whole time talking about books, but nothing about law.

Twenty years ago a young girl turned up at the office asking if we had a job for her. She had a winsome smile and, more noticeably the same surname as mine (though she was no relation). On those slender qualifications we gave her a job. Two decades later Julie has now become my secretary, and has joined the long line of others who despair at the mountains of paper that grow on my desk.

I find that I usually make up my mind within about 30 seconds whether a candidate should have a job. Occasionally I get it wrong. One successful candidate burst into tears on his first day and sobbed for a week until, several buckets full of tears later, he gave it up as a bad job and went off to train as an accountant.

I can however see what the DIY store was getting at, but I think that the technique should be adapted for solicitors. Instead of pulling faces they should be encouraged at the interview to purse their lips (excellent training for the judiciary later in life) and to show there is absolutely no question of discrimination on grounds of anything, each should be required to dance the Gay Gordons. Besides a little waving of arms would give early warning of a potential latter day Miss Whiff.

Chapter 30:
Call out Barr the plumber

Originally published 20 July 2007

"That's a lot of money. I am a solicitor and even I do not charge at that rate."

"That's why I gave up being a solicitor," replied the plumber.

That old joke acquired new significance when we recently had our central heating boiler mended. For remarkably little time on the job we were suddenly several hundred pounds the poorer.

Barr the Plumber – Day One

When our rather delicate female cat spent a night out, and later started to bulge we discovered that once again we needed the services of a plumber.

There is a cavity underneath the hot water tank at the end of the house that has become an occasional maternity ward. It has seen the safe delivery into this world of two litters of Labradors, one pigeon and a nest of mice. The last was unintended and to prevent further illegal immigration we had the cavity boarded up. But there was nowhere else to provide a safe sanctuary for a pregnant cat and, using a crowbar I re-opened the cavity, and incidentally released some pent-up rage against a client from hell who has been making my life a misery.

It was then that I discovered that the tank had sprung a small leak and the whole area was not only damp but had also become a fertile breeding ground for some rare fungi that were in the process of planning to devour the whole house. The source of the leak was the immersion heater. A little tightening should do the trick I thought.

The effect was dramatic. My action released a small torrent which threatened to inundate the ground floor of the house. The more I tightened, the greater the flow. I felt like the Sorcerer's Apprentice, but without the comfort of knowing that the Sorcerer would return to make it all better. I raced around the house trying to find the stopcock and the water was beginning to rival the Yorkshire floods by the time I managed to turn off the supply.

But what to do now? The sensible answer would be to call out a plumber, but I was not about to give in that easily. Surely, I reasoned, a solicitor with many years of experience should be able to do something as straightforward as repair a water leak. After all, Tesco law is encouraging the public to do our job. You don't need a working knowledge of the Statutes of the Realm to join up a few pipes – though of course plumbers should be versed in the implications of *Rylands v Fletcher*.

I had cracked the tank, and the only solution was to replace it. Still confident in my abilities I set off for the nearest DIY superstore and was soon back with what looked like an identical replacement. Easy, you don't need a plumber just to undo the connections and replace the tank.

Wrong. Disconnecting the old one was not as easy as it seemed. My little collection of bicycle spanners was not up to unscrewing the seized pipes.

My second trip to the DIY store yielded a most offensive weapon – a wrench capable of undoing underwater pipelines. With the terrible screech of rending metal I was able to sever the corroded umbilical cords. Even though I had drained the tank, it still contained enough saturated lime scale to leave a thick trail to the back door.

Above the tank was a redundant metal flue. It looked easy to dismantle, so why not? Twenty minutes later there was a loud rumble as many generations of soot, twigs and dead birds dumped onto my head and spread towards the rest of the house like ash from the St Helens eruption. My white limescale path became black. I was already in trouble for leaving footprints on the best carpet and on what turned out to be a priceless chair that I stood on to facilitate my wrestling with the plumbing. The disapproval level was raised to homicidal. So ended my first day as a plumber and my achievements included: a seriously stained carpet, a wrecked chair and no hot water in the house.

Day Two

Whistling tunelessly and demanding cups of tea with six sugars, I connected up the direct supply pipes and then turned to the indirect heating pipes (fellow plumbing solicitors will know what I am talking about). Misery! In the intervening years someone had redesigned hot water tanks with these pipes spaced further apart. The existing pipes did not reach the new connections.

I needed new pipe and elbow joints. Visit number three to the DIY shop provoked a sucking in of teeth. "You have imperial pipes and we only do metric now," said the men behind the counter in unison. "Adaptor? No call for them mate. You could try sanding the pipes to make them compatible but we wouldn't advise it. Very tricky things copper pipes."

But necessity had to be the mother of invention. My rating in the family was rock bottom. After grappling for hours with olives and elbow joints I eventually achieved a connection that would have delighted Mr Heath Robinson. Then came the refilling of the tank. With considerable gurgling the water level reached the top and... started to leak from three different places. I set about the problem with the mighty wrench. It was then that I saw stars. I had left a hammer on a shelf, and my efforts caused it to slide off and fall my head.

I am nothing if not terrified of the consequences of failure, so I was not about to let a little concussion interrupt my struggle to stem the leaks the water kept pouring out.

Back at the DIY shop for the fourth or fifth time, I scoured the shelves for something to stop leaks. Jointing compound seemed to be the answer to my prayer, but on the label it said that I needed a hank of hemp to put between the joints.

The checkout operator took one look at me and fled to her supervisor. It was only later that I realised that the blow on my head had knocked a hole in my skull. I did not realise but the side of my face was bloodstained. Little wonder that she was a little disturbed when someone looking like an extra in a horror movie was asking for hemp.

The leaks eventually stopped. My wife is still cleaning the carpets and the chair is beyond repair. The whole process took two days, but I now have the immense satisfaction of knowing that I have done down one more greedy plumber. All the same, I think I will need a little more practice before I change careers.

"Darling," said my wife gently, as she surveyed my battle scars and the carnage I had caused, "We have a new light fitting to put up. Perhaps we should contact an electrician."

"What and pay their exorbitant rates? They charge more than I do."

"Yes, but the house may still be standing by the time they finish."

And the cat decided – "There is no way I am going to give birth to my kittens in that place" – and promptly made a nest in a drawer at the opposite end of the house.

Chapter 32:
Fired!

Published 25 November 2008

Most of my pieces talk of good times and bad times, but there has been an underlying thread of optimism throughout. But not any more – at least for the time being. I am very shortly to become a statistic.

It happened on Thursday, as the clocks wound their hands round to 5pm. I was tired, and was planning to put my heap of unsorted papers into a neat pile and to set out through the Norfolk gloom to a relatively early evening.

There was something about the expression on the face of my partner that alerted me. He was smiling but the smile was not quite right. Nor was it usual for him to come into my room at that time of night and sit down – still less to close the door behind him: doors are seldom closed in the office.

"The partners have decided…" he began. And I knew the rest. Ever since my quirky and unconventional return (after some years dabbling in multiparty cases) to the firm, I had been struggling to rebuild a clinical negligence practice. And indeed I had – but the problem with such cases is that if you do them on a no-win-no-fee basis you do not get paid until the end – and the end takes years to come. I thought I could turn in a profit after two years. I was wrong, but after three years it is beginning to come good – but not soon enough for the partners. In one day last week 20,000 people lost their jobs. I have now made it 20,001.

Many high-street firms with a mixed practice are haemorrhaging at the moment. The housing market has collapsed; even probates (which you would think would be recession-proof) have tailed off, and of course commercial activity has declined almost to zero. People literally cannot afford to get divorced, because there is no way of realising what is often the main asset (the home). Fee incomes are dramatically below target. But what has not reduced are the overheads of running a practice. Firms across the country are seeing their bank balances drain away and even those prudent firms that did not run on bank loans are having to go cap in hand to their bankers – just at a time when banks are wary of lending money to anyone. It is a dire situation and those who thought they were reasonably secure in their jobs are no longer so. Like me.

I am writing this from the heart because every day hundreds more in the legal profession are going to be in exactly the same position and will, like me, be facing the prospect of a life without the security of knowing that the mortgage will be paid or that there will be something left for the necessities in life.

So what's to be done? At the moment I am still at the 'rabbit in the headlights' stage. I had a long drive home and during that drive I was running the gamut of human emotion – anger, despair, defiance, hope, then more despair. I had already given my long-suffering wife two barrels of grief, so I turned my attention to others as I drove, ringing anyone who might not put the phone down on me. But it did help. Slowly ideas began to crystallise.

Here is stage one of the Richard Barr guide to not panicking when you too get that ruefully smiling visit from a partner late in the afternoon.

There is nothing to be ashamed of. We are in a situation that is completely outside our control. It is not our fault that those who run the banks and financial institutions are so inept that they have precipitated the biggest financial downturn for nearly a hundred years.

We worked to get where we are in our jobs and we must not equate what has happened with our failure. Think what the situation would be if there had been no downturn. We would still be in our jobs (or at least you would – I don't know about myself).

So what's to do?

First, take advice. You may have a long time out of work. Make sure you get what you are entitled to. Remember the old adage that the solicitor who represents himself has a fool for a client. Consider going direct to counsel rather than instructing your own solicitors. You may save a penny or two that way.

Second, use your friends and contacts. It is probably worse than hopeless to apply for jobs at the moment, even if there are any. But someone you have met in your career might know of a niche in a niche practice. Solicitors will not disappear altogether – at least I don't think so. There will still be new jobs somewhere – perhaps related to the very thing that is causing job losses.

Third take stock of your life. Do you really want to be a solicitor for ever? I tell people that I have not yet decided what I want to do when I grow up. Now may be the time to grow up. Consider sole practice. One of the kind people who wrote to me after hearing my news said: "Speaking as a sole practitioner, why don't you set up as a sole practitioner? Then you will never be let down again. I practise from home and have done for the past 14 years. I am not a millionaire but it is a lot nicer life."

Sole practice has become a dirty word in the minds of some. But maybe partnership is a dirty word too. Perhaps there is a halfway stage. Some firms are pioneering what are essentially virtual solicitors' offices, where you work at home but are still part of the firm. That might suit some.

It may not even be worth, at the moment, applying for any job. If you can afford to do so, take a year off. One firm dealing in overland holidays is offering a discount to anyone who produces a recent P45. By the time you return the recession may be over.

Oh, and whatever you do, don't cancel your subscription to *Solicitors Journal*. Otherwise you won't find out what happens next.

[Richard is still a solicitor; he talks about how he picked himself up in Down Under *but not out, page 99]*.

Chapter 33:
Growing old disgracefully

Originally published 13 January 2009

I don't suppose I am the only one who spent much of his adolescence regarding his acne and thinking: *to hell with the ugly duckling story, this one was definitely not going to turn into a swan*. Then adulthood came and I realised that I was no worse looking (and no better) than most of my fellow male law students. Photographs taken at the time show a spindly youth with a thick mound of dark hair and wearing glasses in a heavy black frame giving me a faintly intellectual look – which has long since disappeared. And that was about the last time I bothered too much about my appearance, so don't worry: this is not an exercise in narcissism.

Peel away the acne, broaden the girth, add a few wrinkles and hey presto you land in 2009, but the problem with growing older is that the *you* that looks out lags well behind the *you* that others look at.

So with my mind stuck somewhere between 20 and 30 I fancifully imagine that others would look on me in that light too. But when I do see my reflection in the mirror, the face that looks back has gradually come to resemble an older brother, an uncle and lately a grandfather (although I quickly add that unless my children are hiding something from me, I have not yet achieved that status).

For me the defining moment came when I reached 60. I still did not feel old, but decided that I might as well reap the benefits of that particular landmark – like applying for a Senior Railcard. As instructed, I arrived at the railway station armed with documentation to prove just how old I was. I fancied that I would have to work hard to prove my age. I handed my application to the 16-year-old behind the counter and started to fish out my birth certificate and passport.

"No need," she said, "I won't have to see those," as she handed me my card. May I make a small plea to those who run rail companies: no matter how ancient the applicant for a rail card appears to be, please humour us by training your staff to gasp, shake their heads and declare that they would never have thought you were anything like that old. It would ensure a lasting loyalty to the railways and a tolerance of the service no matter how mediocre.

It means now that these days not only policemen, nurses and doctors are younger than I am but also all cabinet ministers, the last two Prime Ministers, all newsreaders and even the President of the Law Society.

These thoughts were all rammed home before Christmas on the occasion of the Annual General Meeting of the West Norfolk and King's Lynn Law Society. The business of the meeting over, some indifferent wine and beer were served and a little huddle of my generation of solicitors formed an enclave not too far from the waiting bottles of refreshment. There were four of us and we were all around the same age. We had all spent most of our formative years in King's Lynn and had been friendly rivals over several decades. We had seen off previous recessions and survived them. We had also moved from an era where simply being a solicitor was a guarantee of a reasonable income to the present time where two of the four of us have recently had to move jobs because of force of circumstance.

Despite the dark pall of gloom hanging over the AGM, our thoughts were elsewhere. Like elderly patients in a waiting room we chose to talk instead about our health. The youngest in our group had suffered a pulmonary embolism during the previous year. We paused to make the right sympathetic noises before the next told how he was working on top of a ladder and managed to fall off, knocking himself out in the process. Even several days later he still could not remember what had happened.

"That was nothing", the third solicitor said. "I fell off my bike on an icy road and found myself sliding towards a large lorry." He has been riding a bicycle in town for as long as I can remember, never bothering to wear a cycling helmet: his felt hat had served him well so far and he wasn't going to change now. After his fall he was much more concerned about his hat and the lights on his bike than his general well-being. By the time they had all related their health stories everyone started to drift away but nobody asked me about my health problem – which was the most bizarre of all: one day I was walking down the street and found I was seeing through people; apparently an unusual form of migraine.

Growing old is not difficult: all you do is wait and it happens by itself. The trick is to carry on doing so by not falling off ladders or cycling under large vehicles. But whatever the outward appearance, you do not have to act old. Waiting at the opticians the other day to collect my wife I watched the old people walk by, hunched, leaning on sticks, cloth caps on their heads. Simultaneously I realised two things: first, that they were all probably no older than me, and second, that I had an almost uncontrollable desire to rush out and trip them up. If I had, I wonder whether the 16-year-old girl who sold me my senior railcard might have been persuaded at last that whatever I looked like, I was at least not acting 60. Probably not: she would have concluded that I had become senile.

Chapter 34:
Down Under but not out

Originally published 3 March 2009

"I can't possibly go, it is much too soon. I can't. I can't. Anyway, we can't afford it." This, to my wife who wanted so much to see her doctor daughter in Australia after a six-month separation. Her to me still in a state of turmoil after losing my job: "But you must. You've not had a proper holiday for well over a year and if you don't come I will go alone."

So, among all the other pressures that have piled up like so much manure produced by a team of horses, I agreed, regretted it and back-tracked, then caved in and agreed again.

Before Christmas I told the story of my abrupt fall from grace from being a once secure partner in a firm of solicitors to joining the burgeoning ranks of unemployed solicitors (see *Fired*, page 93).

So here is instalment two. After fulminating for many days and feeling angry and extremely sorry for myself I realised that at my time in life I might not be the most appealing candidate for job interviews, but more to the point that I could really do without partners breathing words down my neck like 'targets', 'under-performance' and 'parasite'. In fairness, they did not use the last – but it felt like it.

Going it alone has real drawbacks – not least the almost prohibitive cost of indemnity insurance and the fact that sole practitioners are treated in some quarters as being the legal equivalent of a bad smell. But there was another possibility. Call it a virtual solicitors' office or a sole practitioner's dream, but the reality is that there are firms springing up that challenge the old idea of chaining fee earners to office desks, targets and time recording. One such firm is the one I have joined, Scomo.com, which provides no-frills premises plus infrastructure, insurance and compliance mechanisms to enable those who would be happy never again to be a partner in a firm – not to be.

So how does it work? You join the firm as a self-employed consultant. The support services are provided in return for the firm receiving a percentage (usually 30 per cent) of your fees when they are paid.

Whether you live in Lands End, Llandudno or Lanzarote, all communications are to and from the firm's office in London. This causes no delay because all incoming post is scanned and emailed to fee-earners on the same day.

Fee-earners join 'units' for the purpose of training and supervision, with regular meetings to discuss marketing, strategy and problems.

If you have no clients you will be waiting for a very long time for any income. Consider doing a deal with your firm that enables you not only to take your cases but also your work in progress (after all, your former partners probably said to you that the cases you so cherished were not worth a hill of beans, so offer them a small hill of beans to take them off their hands).

You still have to find a way of staving off bankruptcy while you wait for cases to arrive then finish, and that means setting up business finance. Not a problem, you might think. After all, had not your bank and every credit card company you ever dealt with tumbled over themselves to lend you thousands? Yes they may have done, but that was before you lost your job and the recession kicked in – the past was the past and the future is another country.

My first effort at a business plan failed. Banks want cash flow forecasts and lots of information about how you will eventually earn money. They do not know about conditional fee agreements and the costs rules. I had to prepare a complete DIY kit on personal injury cases to educate the bank into differentiating between me and the man who wants to set up a business breeding alpacas. Eventually, extremely reluctantly, the computer said 'yes', but not before it demanded a first charge on my property, my wife's bees, my fire engine and my mother-in-law.

Then you have to run your cases – from home. Many of us have worked from home from time to time, but this usually means bringing a bulging briefcase home on a Friday, feeling guilty all weekend for not doing the work and, at about 11 pm on Sunday, doing an hour's frantic dictation.

But what if it is not a bulging briefcase but a carload of files, and there is no secretary to type, file, put in envelopes, soothe the clients and you?

Back to the present, and as you will guess 'she who must be obeyed' prevailed. Some things however do not change. I was nowhere near ready to leave by the time we were nearly an hour past our chosen time to leave for the airport. As I ran out of the door with my hastily packed suitcase, I was still stuffing letters into envelopes and putting the finishing touches to letters that I hoped would cause my opposite numbers to go weak at the knees.

And now I am sitting with my laptop in Federation Square in Melbourne with the late Australian summer sun filling with warmth the unaccustomed crevices in my pale skin, and I am thinking that I am after all glad I came.

But wait, an email has just flashed up on my screen – a letter from some defendants: "Dear Sirs, Upon receipt of your letter we went weak at the knees and we admit liability."

Sorry folks, must dash. Work calls.

Chapter 35:
Tea with the Queen

Originally published 29 July 2009

A few weeks ago –

There were a few corgis lapping around her ankles. She was sitting at a desk with a very large tome on it filled with lists of names of her subjects, all written in copperplate hand. She paused at one of the names, then reached for a bell push.

In the distance was the faint sound of tinkling. A few moments later a distinguished man appeared in the room and negotiated his way past the corgis.

"Ah, Simkins," she said, "I have come across the name of the Barr family from Norfolk. I would like to invite them to tea. I command you to deal with it please."

"Yes, Maam," replied Simkins, for she was the Monarch and he was the Lord Chamberlain.

"And while you are about it, could you round up another 7,996 guests. I wouldn't want the Barrs to feel self-conscious if they were the only ones."

"Indeed, Maam."

"Oh, and Simkins," – the distinguished man turned and bowed – "Could you pop down to the Mace shop and get some biscuits for Princess" (here she nodded at a corgi that was lying on a chaise longue).

And so it came to pass, that last month the postman delivered a vellum envelope of the most expensive kind containing an invitation that will grace our mantelpiece until it turns yellow with age.

It said: "The Lord Chamberlain is commanded by Her Majesty to invite…" us.

In the ensuing weeks the ladies kitted themselves out in hats and elegant dresses. And it was made clear that I needed a makeover myself – like the acquisition of a new suit ("no not another one that costs £50. And those shoes. You cannot go there in those shoes. She will think you are the gardener.") The list went on: shirt, tie, even underwear – despite my protests that it was pretty unlikely that I would be required to strip down to my Y-fronts.

Came the appointed day, there was pandemonium in the Barr household as we struggled to get ready – then panic as we set out late for London, terrified that if we did not make it in time we would be BARRed.

In the nick of time we reached the Mall, lined with smiling police officers. There were four of us – Kirsten my wife, and two of her daughters Bryony (who is in a wheel chair), tall willowy Philippa, and me whose only claim to fame is that I was appointed to the Council of the Law Society because no one else wanted to represent Norfolk. The Law Society is one of many organisations that can nominate guests for one of the Queen's garden parties – and our name came out of the hat.

Did I say 'hat'? There were thousands of them – ladies' hats of all colours shapes and sizes and men's top hats, military hats and caps, traditional native headgear and senior officers whose hats had enough gold in the braid to rescue the economy.

"And what part of the world are you from?" – this, from a 60-something man with a well travelled face, a top hat on his head and a carnation in his button hole.

We were standing next to an enormous marquee where immaculate staff were pouring tea from highly polished kettles, and symmetrical sandwiches and little cakes bearing the royal crest were piled high on salvers. In front, in the bright July sunshine, the hats waved and danced as those underneath them sat at tables and consumed the Royal feast.

Thinking that I ought to know the 60-something man, I kept talking, introducing him to the family and mentioning in passing that Bryony, who has disabilities, had cherished the ambition to meet the Queen. At this, he produced some cards from his pocket and proceeded to write down our details using his top hat to rest the paper.

"This is about the only thing these things are good for," he explained as he wrote. "Right, leave it with me and I will see what I can do. Meet me at the second urn on the left," indicating towards the Palace.

As it happens, we were not welcome at the second urn on the left. We were soon seen off by a large axe-bearing beafeater who told us we were not allowed on the gravel.

By then our 7,996 fellow guests had been parted into long avenues. Our man, who turned out to be a 'gentleman usher', lined us up, slightly jutting out from the rest of the crowd. Then suddenly the band struck up the national anthem.

Slowly the Queen processed down our avenue. As each family was presented to her, she was briefed by the real Lord Chamberlain – who is not called Simkins. All the while she was followed at a discreet distance by a phalanx of ladies-in-waiting and other staff who crept forward as the Queen did, only moving when her back was turned, as though they were playing a royal game of grandmother's footsteps.

Then our turn came. The Queen, dressed in bright pink, was smaller than I imagined and looked much younger than her 83 years. She was interested and soft spoken. We talked about Norfolk and she said that she had recently returned from there: "One likes to go there in different seasons," she explained, and I had to remind myself that she did not just have a quaint country cottage there.

Then Bryony realised her dream as the Queen bent down and greeted her.

Chapter 36:
Smoke signals

Originally published 8 June 2010

Don't think you can escape that easily. When you retire from the stress of the office to tend your roses do not expect a peaceful life, for the anxiety caused by a sick rose causes no less angst than the managing partner visiting you with crocodile smile and telling you that for the third month running you failed to meet your target. So what is it like if you have not retired *and* you still have to tend your roses?

It is therapeutic to experience the suffering of others. We always slow down to rubber neck the aftermath of a road accident (and some of us of course take the opportunity to toss out a few business cards to the victims as they sit on the road side). Similarly it is fun at election time to see the politicians you loved to hate being made to walk away into the sunset. So for your pleasure go ahead and enjoy this year's crop of Barr disasters.

The haunting melody started to trickle from my right thigh. As usual it always happens at inconvenient moments – on this occasion, at the super-market checkout. That particular tone means just one thing. It's my wife calling, and I will be in trouble if I ignore her.

The message was simple and in some households might not have been surprising: "On your way out, can you get me a packet of cigarettes". It has been a stressful time for her lately, what with the accident with the bees and the great chicken massacre, not to mention the invasion of crows. But to the best of my knowledge neither of us has ever smoked.

It was a while back that I came out of the front door one bright sunny morning to see Kirsten lying in the grass. Even to my unobservant nature there was something amiss about her taking a nap in the grass so early in the day. Further investigation revealed that she was not alone. Lying beside her was a step ladder with a bent leg, and on top of her were about 20,000 bees and a cardboard box.

Eventually she sat up with bees circling her in a good imitation of the stars that orbit cartoon characters when they are clubbed on the head.

She had been trying to catch a swarm and had climbed to the top of an unsecured step ladder, holding the box above her to entrap the bees. You can imagine the rest.

Even with the mother and father of all headaches, it still took a week to persuade her to go to her doctor who ordered her to hospital immediately with the most effective referral letter in medical history: "*Please see this lady who has suffered a head injury. Her husband is a clinical negligence lawyer and her daughter is a brain surgeon*" (both true).

Within a nanosecond of our arrival at A&E she had been shown into a cubicle where a consultant was waiting for her – who not only took charge of her case but personally wheeled her to the radiology department for a CT scan. Fortunately it was all clear, but that referral is a technique I recommend if you are a penniless lawyer and cannot afford to go private.

Following the arrival of the ducks last year our garden has now been granted the coveted Golden Bill Award by the Mallard Times. Last year's crop of ducklings eventually shed their downy feathers and grew into real ducks. Despite the predictions of the RSPCA (to whom we turned when we felt we were being overrun) they did not leave in the winter. Not only did they not leave, they also invited their mates. Throughout the spring, successive mother ducks have arrived at our pond with delicious yellow ducklings which were soon spotted by the crows that occupy the taller trees.

In an attempt to forestall the inevitable massacre we placed two stuffed birds of prey on long bendy poles and tied plastic bags on others. For about half a day this fooled the crows (it puzzled the neighbours for longer) until they decided that this was a further invitation to have duckling for tea. The upshot is that, as I type this, there is but one nervous duckling on the pond. There is also a salivating crow looking down on it.

This gets too depressing. Just accept that we went into chickens this year. We started with five. They were very sweet and sang to you as they demonstrated that they are the first creatures in our household actually to earn their keep. But then, along came the fox. Now the surviving chickens live behind an electrified fence which has so far defied the foxes.

Let me give you a tip if you are a man. If you choose to step over an electric fence, do make sure you are well insulated between the legs or you might end up sparking in places that you would rather not.

Which of course brings me back to the roses. Feeling about as self conscious as a teenager asking for a condom I approached the tobacco kiosk and bought the cheapest and most dangerous cigarette pack.

So – Kirsten was not about to smoke. All she wanted to do was poison the green fly on the roses with cigarette fumes. That's a relief. Still, after the stresses of spring, I think I might take the pack behind the bicycle shed to calm my nerves. Perhaps after my encounter with the electric fence it might help to stop me speaking in a high-pitched voice. And then maybe I can get back to doing a bit of law – for a rest.

Chapter 37:
Normal for Norfolk

Originally published 10 August 2010

Bill Bryson, the travel writer, confessed in one of his early books that he came from Iowa because "somebody had to".

Sometimes it feels the same about Norfolk where I come from – or at least where I have been for the last 40 years: somebody had to come from Norfolk.

You sense just the slight hint of a sneer – often no more than the flicker of a moustache or the twitch of an eyebrow – when you mention to those who consider that they live in more sophisticated counties like Sussex or Hampshire, that you hail from Norfolk.

Then almost immediately they remember the line from Noel Coward's *Private Lives*: "Very flat, Norfolk".

And when, not many years ago, Martin Mears disrupted the smooth flow of succession in the Law Society by getting himself elected President, one council member described him as a backwoodsman and a legal journal (not this one) called him a Norfolk Yokel. I am sure that if he had come from Gloucestershire he would automatically have been treated with the respect we accord to all our presidents.

So what is wrong with Norfolk and why does it attract comments like this? Why do doctors enter the acronym NFN in medical notes when they want to say "Normal for Norfolk" (often accompanied by TATSP – thick as two short planks)?

There is, it has to be admitted, a certain impenetrability about some Norfolk people. The more you chatter nervously to them, the more they go quiet, fixing you with that kind of stare that car mechanics reserve for those who insist that their new car has a rattle.

I once sat on a committee in a village in the heart of Norfolk which had a five-star rating in the Domesday Book and has changed little since William the Conqueror's inspectors left.

The committee members, all men, would sit for long periods in complete silence, and only occasionally would one of their number make a point before lapsing back into wordlessness. I was not about to break the mould, so I, too, went to these gatherings and never uttered a word. Invariably the chairman would end each meeting by thanking us all for our contributions.

Sidney Grapes, the eccentric pre-war Norfolk comedian summed it up: "You can always tell a Norfolk man, but you can't tell him much."

Many have had their say about the county. Novelist Raffaella Barker: "*the freedom of a place where more than 50 per cent of the neighbours are fish*", and Reginald Pound, author of Scott of the Antarctic: "*It is littered with villages but uncluttered by towns*".

And there is the Norfolk saying which is just as applicable today as it has always been: "*Norfolk is cut off on three sides by the sea and on the fourth by British Rail.*" It is no longer British Rail but the rail company of the moment regularly ensures that those who dare to venture out of Norfolk will find themselves admiring the trackside litter from a stationary train not many miles outside Norwich. Travelling by car is little better. The county does not have one inch of motorway and the powers that be have ensured that the main route out of the county (the A11) is permanently congested on the Suffolk border where it narrows to a single carriage way. I think that in conveyancing terms this is called a ransom strip. It keeps them out and us in.

If you come from one of those well heeled and sophisticated counties I have already mentioned and think we are thick and backward, you had better think again: if it weren't for us in Norfolk there would not be any of you in your posh counties.

Visible from where we live is the red-and-white striped lighthouse at Happisburgh (pronounced 'Haysbro') which was some years ago given a lick of paint by Anneka Rice as she was flying around in her helicopter (or perhaps she was on dry land then).

That lighthouse is slowly creeping towards the sea, or, more accurately, the sea is creeping towards it, because the tall cliffs in the village are crumbling fast. Already several homes have gone over the edge.

Encroachment of the sea has nonetheless provided valuable information to archaeologists and evidence that the first known human settlement in northern Europe was here in Happisburgh on the North Norfolk coast.

In short, Norfolk is the cradle of British civilisation. Furthermore, the river Thames at that time flowed past Happisburgh. The village website for a while renamed itself "Happisburgh on Thames."

All those years ago, the good people of Happisburgh on Thames were no doubt living in much the same way as those who are now in the Home

Counties. Archaeologists will soon be reporting as they dig deeper that early Norfolk people had laptops, fast cars and aircraft made out of carbon fibre; that they lived in skyscrapers (resembling striped lighthouses) and walked on the moon. It was only when they were overthrown by the barbarians from Sussex, Hampshire and Gloucester that they died out, apart from a small number who had to pretend they were TATSP in order to conceal their intellectual superiority.

And so it remains today. If you get the slightest impression that any of us are a little thick, you will be entirely mistaken. We are simply deep in thought refining Einstein's Law of Relativity so that it embraces quantum physics and dark matter. And for good reason: Einstein took refuge in Norfolk after fleeing Nazi Germany and lived for a while in a hut near Cromer.

Chapter 38:
Space man

Originally published 12 July 2011

It was not like any court I had appeared in before. The judge towered above us from a raised dais. Even though he looked like a giant octopus and had at least three eyes I am sure he was a judge because he had an impressive wig on his head.

He busied himself dealing with various administrative matters. He had so many tentacles that this appeared to be an easy task. Perhaps the judge was really 'she' because there was a considerable amount of multitasking – sorting out what appeared to be documents, completing forms, pressing buttons on a giant console and making noises into what I took to be some sort of telephone.

I and several obese people, a small dog, a hedgehog and an unhappy gold fish in a polythene bag stood in the well of the court. We had all come here by the same route. I think there were more of us. I am sure I saw a horse and wasn't that the chairman of the local parish council who joined us after the people from the trailer park – and the butterfly?

It was my fault really. I had been looking at one of those forms that are sent out to worry solicitors. It was a business continuity checklist.

That sounds innocuous but what it really meant was for us each to say how we would be able to carry on calmly doing the things that calm solicitors do when the sea water is up to the eaves, or when an earthquake of 8.1 on the Richter scale has razed the house.

We have to demonstrate that as the flames are licking around us we will continue to be able to dictate on our fire proof dictating machines and pore over files that are filled with flame retardant paper and key in our all-important time recording units onto computer hard drives that can still operate from two miles under the sea or in the kind of heat that melts pig iron.

Against the business continuity criteria my idea that I could keep my life's work on a portable hard drive in my pocket seemed to be a solution of sorts.

Taking a break from form filling I made the mistake of watching one of the television programmes that prove that we have aliens living among us and that governments are covering up the truth.

There was a time when these aliens concentrated their efforts on the inhabitants of US trailer parks but there has been a worrying shift recently: now respectable airline pilots, bank clerks, nurses and policemen are all reporting sightings of saucer-shaped objects that fly at impossible speeds and appear and disappear in an instant.

And that is why it came to be my turn to be abducted. It was between Letheringsett and Holt, just on the corner by the bridge, where if the bells are ringing in the church you get an impressive Doppler shift as you drive by.

One minute I was listening to the dropping note of the bells and the next minute I had joined the small crowd inside the saucer-shaped object that was sitting on the road. We moved off at break neck speed and were soon travelling so fast that we could see planet Thong approaching through the porthole.

The saucer let us out into a pleasant place that smelled slightly of fish that had passed its sell-by date.

The traffic seemed to consist of small flying saucers looking a little like bubble cars without wheels. They were all driven by the same sort of creature as the judge but smaller.

Our saucer had arrived on the steps of the court. Disconcertingly it looked like the now defunct Cromer magistrates court. Two octopi wearing policemen's helmets directed us inside. One of the fat people demurred and was given a quick swipe with a long tentacle. After that the rest of us, including the hedgehog and the butterfly, meekly obeyed.

The judge then opened his mouth (or one of them) and addressed me in quaint English.

"Forsooth Mr Barr, verily we have brought you here for a purpose".

"How did you know my name?" I spluttered.

"Yea, do not interrupt. Our tentacles reach a long way". He waved one of them to emphasise the point. "We have brought you here because in the intergalactic issue of *Solicitors Journal* you therein did refer to one of our kind Jonathan Djanogly [at the time a parliamentary Under Secretary of State at the Ministry of Justice]. We want him back but we do not know his whereabouts."

"That's easy," I replied, and gave him directions to the Houses of Parliament, suggesting that the saucer could land on the terrace by the Thames. I added that he was very welcome to have him back, and would he be interested in Ken Clarke at the same time?

"I am deeply indebted to you," he made a kind of bow, "now if you are quick you can catch the 4.30 saucer back to your depressing little planet".

Hours later I was back in my car and still between Letheringsett and Holt. I rang my wife to try to explain why I had been delayed. She sounded nonplussed and pointed out that I had only called two minutes earlier from the same location.

"It's a long story" I said. And left it at that. Then I suddenly realised that I had left my pocket hard drive and my jacket on planet Thong. Now how do I recover from that disaster?

Chapter 39:
Pillock in tassels

Originally published 18 October 2011

While the world was watching the face of Amanda Knox in the final moments of her appeal in the desperately sad case of the murder of Meredith Kercher, I was like a cat fascinated by a piece of string, because the television pictures would from time to time pan across the court to reveal the attire of the Italian lawyers.

I know that in dignified situations, one's dress must match the occasion, but why were the lawyers wearing curtain tassels sticking out of their arms?

What we wear defines us, as I found out recently when I was subjected to a humiliating, but interesting, experience in a clothes store in Norwich.

We are now about to enter a new era, if the doom-laden views expressed in a recent newspaper article are to be believed. *The Times* reported the predictions of one investment bank that virtually all the ten thousand or so firms of high street solicitors will close down because they will either be pushed out of business or absorbed into larger firms or 'Tesco Law' once alternative business structures go live.

High street solicitors will need to find survival techniques in the brave new world of ABS. And the first thing we will need to do is get ourselves noticed.

It does not take much to assume an air of authority. Two men meet in the street. One has shoulder epaulettes and the other (a solicitor) does not. The man with the epaulettes is instantly more noticeable, so the solicitor goes to his local epaulette shop and the following day strolls down the high street with brand new epaulettes. To his chagrin, coming the other way is a woman with a blue blazer and the golden chevrons of an airline pilot on her sleeve. Once again the solicitor is trumped, so that evening he pays a visit to his chevron shop. Proudly he displays his chevrons the following day but he is met by the airline pilot this time wearing a braided peaked cap. At this point the solicitor goes to his local army surplus store and emerges with peaked cap encrusted with scrambled egg, epaulettes, golden braid and as many medals as he can squeeze onto his chest. This time passers by look on him in pity and press low denomination coins into his hand with a "God bless you sir for winning the war for us, sir".

Cut to Marks and Spencer in Norwich. I had got myself into one of those situations I wished I had managed to avoid. I was talking a little law on BBC Radio Norfolk when we were joined by a fashion expert who had come to discuss autumn clothes for women and men. Nowadays you do not put on a dinner jacket to appear on the radio, so I had shown up in jeans. The presenter and fashion expert then turned on me and announced to the world (or at least to the local radio listeners) that they would take me to the local shops to give me a makeover.

A few weeks later I found myself on the radio being described as having the John Major look as I was so grey that I would be invisible to almost everyone who passed me in the street. It was all apparently down to vibration and wavelength and grey was not a good wavelength to transmit.

I was first given the casual look, with a pink chequered shirt worn outside a pair of jeans rolled up at the ankles (to make me look slimmer). Over my shoulders was a kind of cardigan with leather buttons and on my head had been placed a flat cap.

"I look a pillock," I said to the people of Norfolk.

Then I had to be more formal and on went a dark blue suit, white shirt and striped tie (with grey in the stripes to make me feel at home). I was presented with black shoes that ended in a point. Several toes had to be amputated before I could get my feet into them. I had to acknowledge that this was an improvement: I almost stood out from the background.

A blue suit is not going to save the solicitors' profession and if practitioners are going to survive they are going to have to find more imaginative ways of making themselves known and wanted. I do not necessarily advocate that we don epaulettes or the kind of peaked caps that dictators of small countries wear.

Yet those who dress well are more likely to be listened to than those who wear baggy suits and shirts with frayed cuffs and collars (my normal attire).

So think about curtain tassels on your shoulders. These could become the mark of our trade, just as you recognise your doctor because she has a stethoscope round her neck. We would not then have to worry about meeting people wearing epaulettes or chevrons because everyone will know that those who have dangly curtain tassels on their sleeves are solicitors. They might say we look a bunch of pillocks, but at least we would stand out.

Warning: if we don't do something we will all be wearing the uniforms of supermarkets and serving up three wills for the price of two as we scan their legal wares at the checkout – that is, unless our epaulettes earn us the position of store detectives or we are moved into the curtain department to sell tassels.

Chapter 40:
Frothing sheep

Originally published 21 February 2012

Earlier I wrote an article on the theme *Beware smiling jurors* (see page 16). Now thrill to the case of the smiling sheep.

In the darkness the sheep were showing bright white teeth. I smiled back. It was Sunday – traditionally the day when I give my brain a rest. No, alright, let me say it – the day when I give what is left of my brain a rest.

There were about four inches of snow on the ground. It was cold. I had been chosen to give them their supper because the sheep's owner (my wife) had her feet up as she was recovering from a gruelling drive around the M25 in heavy snow. She is not a delivery driver – though it may come to that if the government does not stop making the lives of ordinary solicitors a misery. She had gone to Heathrow in the first snow of winter to collect her bronzed daughter who had arrived back from Australia in a straw hat and sandals, apparently unaware that in crossing the world the outside temperature had dropped from 32º to -2º.

I looked more closely. Could the white really be snow, not teeth? I brushed against a mouth – it was warm. Not snow. Not a smile at all. Then I panicked – ran into the house shouting "the sheep are foaming at the mouth."

It is an unwritten tenet of sod's law that if a vet is needed the animal in question will fall ill at the most inconvenient hour, when the vet is on double or treble time, and when most normal human beings and animals should be asleep.

For the second time in little over a month it has happened to us. Inevitably the first was on Christmas Day, when one of the cats was apparently looking a little grey. It was actually a grey cat, but was looking greyer than usual. A few days earlier, I saw a rat in the house and decided to feed it poison. The rat then disappeared and the cat started to look grey. Fearing the worst, we raced through dark lanes until we saw a lone glow in the sky. The all night veterinary centre was in full activity – coping with a guinea pig with laryngitis, a budgerigar with indigestion and now a grey cat that was greyer than usual. At the sight of the vet the cat perked up immediately, was seriously affronted when it had its temperature taken and, as the vet relieved me of £100, made a spontaneously complete recovery.

The sheep arrived on the scene a couple of years ago. Farming is not in my blood but I reckoned without the gentle eccentricity of my wife Kirsten who had cherished an ambition to have a small flock of Wensleydale Sheep. To me Wensleydale meant cheese but when these animals arrived they did not resemble cheese at all.

We started with four ewes – sheep with distinctive Rastafarian hairstyles. Apparently four sheep do not make a flock and it was not long before they went to Suffolk for a few weeks of pleasure, as a result of which they all came back with coloured markings on their backs to denote that they had been 'covered' by a ram whose task it was to 'service' a whole flock of sheep. This being a family publication I will withold further detail.

Then along came the lambs and I converted into assistant midwife, helping in about the same ineffectual way that fathers used to in the days gone by when babies were delivered at home. Pat him on the head and tell him to go and boil a kettle.

For a few months the lambs leaped and gambolled, and every one who saw them breathed "Ahhhh, how cute". Then the lambs stopped being lambs and are now fully grown sheep that have absolutely no risk of being turned into chops as they all have names and have become as tame as dogs.

For months the sheep safely grazed and regularly demanded extra food and all was well until last Sunday, when the sheep chose to smile at me. But their kind of smiling meant a late-night call to the vet. It would not have been practical to put 12 large Wensleydale sheep into the back of the car and take them to the glowing lights of the all-night vet. Besides I did not have the £1,200 that it might have cost me.

Looking a little like the latest reincarnation of Dr Who, the vet arrived and diagnosed that the sheep had been supplementing their diets during a snow storm by eating things they ought not have done in the hedgerows, and that their guts now needed balancing.

What was now needed was egg whites and bicarbonate of soda. I don't know if you have ever tried, in freezing cold, to extract egg whites, mix bicarbonate of soda in a bucket and administer it to a dozen foaming sheep. If you have not, I suggest you put it low down on the list of things you would like to do most in 2012. Sheep do not like it, and wrestling with them in the snow on a Sunday night with the Dr Who vet looking on is bad for blood pressure.

So my advice to you is to stick with jurors, but if they start foaming at the mouth, then best to change your submissions or sack your counsel. It may be tough to administer bicarbonate of soda and egg whites to sheep, but I guess it would be well nigh impossible to do so to members of a jury. And what about the judge?

Chapter 41:
Postman Barr

Originally published 15 May 2012

Let me introduce you to Sam, Lyndsey, Del, Sharon, Charlotte and Phyllis. You don't know them, nor are likely to unless you frequent the same small Norfolk market town that I do. However, all will be revealed in the fullness of time.

I had to sign the Official Secrets Act when I started one of my first jobs. I suspect that in writing this piece I may be committing several breaches of the Act, so this could be the last contribution from me as a free man for many years.

It was like this. There used to be a time when stamps were cheap and post was plentiful. Never more was this true than in the weeks leading up to Christmas. In the village of Elm in Cambridgeshire, the local sub post office would recruit child labour to assist in the task of getting the mail out to the good citizens of the village.

I cannot remember how old I was – maybe 16, possibly less. I duly signed up (and signed the Act) and was allocated my mail bag. I had to bring my own bicycle – it was to be many years before those little trolleys were provided.

My patch was to be the Low Road, which ran parallel to the High Road. Everyone who was everyone lived on the High Road and everyone else lived on the Low Road.

My mail had helpfully been sorted so that if I got it right, I started with a full bag at one end and my bag was empty by the time I reached the other end.

Cautiously I set out on my Black Raleigh bicycle, with Sturmey Archer gears (hardly necessary in the Fens as the altitude never varied by more than a few feet, but this was my pre-Macho period so I had to have something to show my manhood).

I was soon to be confronted with a bewildering choice of houses many of which were, in the Fenland tradition where the soil is unstable, leaning at odd angles. There were the usual names that grace any street:

Dunroamin, Shangri-La, Chez Nous, Bide a Wee and Sans Souci. Other houses were probably named after exciting moments in the occupants' lives – El Alamein, Dunkirque and Didcot (no doubt because of pleasant times standing on the railway station there).

With my normal level of competence I managed to deliver many cards to the wrong address but the thing that people particularly objected to was bent calendars. Many had letterboxes with slits no larger than a CD case. There was no way that the average calendar would make it through the letter box to the yapping dog waiting on the other side ready to snatch it, unless it had been bent at least in half. Needless to say Mr Crown the sub-postmaster was not pleased and I received a formal warning before my next round.

So, having failed to become a postman, I did the next best thing and became a solicitor and a deliveree as opposed to a deliveror of mail. That did not always fare well. At an early stage in my career I was in charge of our primitive franking machine and one night franked all the office post at £5 an envelope. Fortunately there were not many letters sent that day (it was the branch office) but it did make a dent in that month's profits for the firm, and probably gave the post office a welcome boost.

The post office has now come in for a lot of flack over its price rises which, it has to be said, are pretty insensitive bearing in mind the economic climate.

Now that I work on my own, stuff my own envelopes, pay for and lick my own stamps, I have a much closer appreciation of the cost of postage than I did when my post went to the post room. A sheet of a hundred first class stamps now costs nearly as much as a tank full of petrol. It is not cheap – or is it?

Imagine what would happen if we had to deliver our own letters. At £200 an hour, and assuming a solicitor walks at four miles an hour, the 60p price of a stamp would get the envelope just 21 yards before the solicitor demanded a further payment on account. Obviously a legal aid solicitor (at £50 an hour) would go four times as far, but even then it would have to be a very local delivery to reach its destination before money ran out. Imagine if a solicitor had to deliver a letter in Cornwall. Even if we were to give him a post van he would still take many hours and would bill at least £1,000.

When I arrive breathless and disheveled at the North Walsham post office at about 5.27pm with my clutch of letters for far flung destinations I am always treated with courtesy and humour by Sam, Lyndsey, Del, Sharon, Charlotte or Phyllis even though I am sometimes the last customer to arrive before closing time.

Sixty pence is a lot for one stamp but I am always pleasantly surprised at how many letters arrive at the right addresses all over the country by the following morning. You get a lot for your 60p. There is also something old-fashioned and special about the counter service at local post offices. The staff are infinitely patient and invariably helpful – even if all you are asking for is proof of posting (which hardly nets a big fee for the organisation). So let's not knock the Post Office, because solicitors would not make good postmen. I know. I've been there.